EVEREST
The Descent

Everest, The Descent
2026 © James Allen

First published February 2026

ISBN 978-1-7640004-0-6 Paperback
ISBN 978-1-7640004-1-3 Epub
ISBN 978-1-7640004-2-0 Audio

A catalogue record for this
book is available from the
National Library of Australia

Book design and production by
exlibris.com.au

EVEREST
The Descent

James Allen

Contents

Background to text and photos in this story

The following text is part of a raw extract from a private tape recording made to my family on the 10th of June 1995, directly after returning to Australia from the climb. Besides a few edits to put events in order and remove repetition, I have left the text largely unaltered.

The "quotes" of the words spoken by climbers at various points are the quotes I used in the tape recording. Some parts do sound like an excited 22-year-old speaking because that's what it is.

A few footnotes have been added where I feel further clarification is required. These notes came from extracts of interviews, newspapers, books and talks given after the expedition and after the tape recording. They serve to help explain the situation at or after that time.

All the photos were taken by me during the expedition using a small Nikon AF600 analogue camera and an instant Fuji print camera, which I carried with me to the summit.

The trip was organised by National Geographic. Their goal was to film a series of renowned climbers climbing a new technical route on Everest. The permits and logistics were coordinated by Out There Travel (OTT) based in Sheffield, England, owned and operated by Jon Tinker and Andy Broom.

Nineteen Western climbers, eight Nepalese Sherpa and three cooks were selected (see Table 1). The Western climbers came from seven countries, Australia, Britain, France, Ireland, Russia, Turkey, and the United States of America. We were selected from hundreds of applicants across the world for our mountaineering skills and ability to work together in a team under stress. While a lot of the trip was paid for by the major sponsors, I still needed to raise about AU$30,000 myself. I did this through generous donations from the sponsors, Ernst & Young, Fuji, Kraft, Arthur Robinson & Hedderwicks, friends and personal savings.

	Name (country)			Name (country)
1	Jon Tinker (Britain), leader	16	Pat Falvey (Ireland)
2	Ang Rita (Nepal), sardar/leader	17	Babu Chiri Sherpa (Nepal)
3	George Kotov (Russia), climbing leader	18	Cook 1 (Nepal)
4	Mike Smith (Britain), climbing leader	19	Cook 2 (Nepal)
5	James Allen (Australia)	20	Cook 3 (Nepal)
6	Kelly Armitage (Australia)	21	Dorji (Nepal)
7	Mick Chapman (Australia)	22	Nima Sherpa 1 (Nepal)
8	Brigitte Muir (Australia)	23	Nima Sherpa 2 (Nepal)
9	Jon Muir (Australia)	24	Lama Jangbu (Nepal)
10	Graham Illing (Britain)	25	Lhakpa Nuru Sherpa (Nepal)
11	Yves Detry (France)	26	Sherpa (Nepal)
12	Patrick Hache (France)	27	Nasuh Mahruki (Turkey)
13	Luc Jourjon (France)	28	Bob Hempstead (USA)
14	Jacques Pouliquen (France)	29	Jeff Shea (USA)
15	Andre Tremoulierre (France)	30	Fred Zalokar (USA)

Table 1. List of all expedition members pre-monsoon March to May 1995

Some facts and figures about Everest before the 1995 pre-monsoon season (March to June)

I climb because I enjoy it. I like the single focus of a difficult move, feeling the rawness and beauty of nature throughout all my senses, and above all, the personal growth I get from testing myself in extreme conditions. I also really like hanging out around campfires and mountain crags with the tribe of people who enjoy the outdoor lifestyle as much as I do.

I started rock climbing in Victoria when I was 14 and mountaineering in New Zealand when I was 20. That was late for most climbers around the world, even then. Like many students, I was financially broke during this time, so much of my climbing was done on first sight without guidebooks. In my mind I always felt like I could climb a route, but in practice many routes that looked easy from below had some challenging section or sections that I had neglected to see from lower down. This confident ignorance did, however, lead me to climb many dangerous routes early on in my career. I didn't mean for this to happen, it was just the way it worked out. Luckily, I survived this period and that, together with my roughnecking on oil rigs in the deserts of Australia, gave me the technical and inter-team qualifications to be selected for the 1995 ascent team.

Statistics have never been a driver for me to do something. Before venturing to Mount Everest, I had little idea about the facts and figures of the mountain, just that few people attempted it and sadly many of them died in the process. Besides that, I also knew that it was high, really high. Since I had never been above 4,500 metres, I had no idea what it meant to be above 8,000 metres.

Some of the statistics up to 1995:

- The North Ridge of Everest was then the deadliest mountaineering route in the world. Fifty-six people had climbed Everest via this route, with thirty dying in the process (slightly more than one death for every two ascents).
- On average one person died per expedition to Everest, with most of those deaths being on the North Col to North East Ridge as the objective route.
- I became the youngest Westerner to ever reach the summit via any of the technical non-South Col routes, the second youngest Westerner to reach the summit of Everest via any route from any side and the tenth youngest person from any nationality to reach the summit (see Table 2).
- I am Australian. However, I do hold three citizenships: Australian (by naturalisation), New Zealand (by descent), United Kingdom (by birth). On reaching the summit I became the youngest Australian, New Zealand and British climber ever to reach the top of Mount Everest via any route at that time.

Rank Age (Westerner North Side)	Rank Age (Westerner all routes)	Rank Age (All North Side)	Rank Age (All all routes)	Age	Name	M/F	Nationality	DOC	Route	Summit Number
1	2	2	10	22	James Allen	M	Australia	May 27, 1995	N Col-NE Ridge	604
2	3	3	11	22	Andrej Stremfelj	M	Yugoslavia	May 13, 1979	Lho La-W Ridge up; N Face (Hornbein)-W Ridge down	84
-	1	-	2	17	Bertrand (Zebulon) Roche	M	France	Oct 7, 1990	S Col-SE Ridge	308
-	4	-	13	22	Ms. Soon-Joo Kim	F	S Korea	May 10, 1993	S Col-SE Ridge	448
-	-	1	3	18	Ngapo Khyen (Abu Qin)	M	China	May 27, 1975	N Col-NE Ridge	43
-	-	4	12	22	Samdrup (Samdruk)	M	China	May 27, 1975	N Col-NE Ridge	45
-	-	-	1	17	Shambu Tamang (Lisankhu, 1955) (1/2)	M	Nepal	May 5, 1973	S Col-SE Ridge	31
-	-	-	4	19	Ms. Dicky Dolma	F	India	May 10, 1993	S Col-SE Ridge	456
-	-	-	5	19	Ms. Radha Devi Thakur	F	India	May 16, 1993	S Col-SE Ridge	476
-	-	-	6	20	Ms. Kunga Bhutia	F	India	May 10, 1993	S Col-SE Ridge	457
-	-	-	7	20	Pasang Kami Sherpa (Kharikhola, 1973) (1/4)	M	Nepal	Oct 7, 1993	S Col-SE Ridge	506
-	-	-	8	21	Ang Jangbu (Ang Jambu) Sherpa (Pangboche, 1958)	M	Nepal	Oct 2, 1979	S Col-SE Ridge	97
-	-	-	9	21	Dawa Tshering Sherpa (Gumela, 1967) (1/2)	M	Nepal	Oct 2, 1988	S Col-SE Ridge	223

Table 2. List of the youngest climbers (including all North Side climbers) to reach the summit of Mount Everest up until 1995. Note the term "Westerner" and "non-Westerner" was used at this time as many climbers from the non-Western countries, such as China, Nepal and India, did not have birth certificates to confirm their date of birth. Many, such as Ngapo Khyen (Abu Qin) from China, did not know their exact year of birth so they or the leaders of their team recorded an educated guess of their age.

You cannot stay on the summit forever;
you have to come down again.
So why bother in the first place?

Just this: what is below does not know what is above.
One climbs, one sees.
One descends, one sees no longer but one has seen.

There is an art of conducting oneself in the lower regions
by the memory of what one has seen higher up.
When one can no longer see, one can at least still know.

René Daumal

To the friends I made on this trip who later died pursuing their love for the outdoors. I will always remember the laughs and love of living for the moment that we shared together.

Alison Hargreaves (33)

Some people climb mountains, but Alison belonged to them. A force of nature in a petite frame, she was the first woman to summit Everest alone and without oxygen. Yet Alison wasn't just a climber, she was a light. In a world of hardened men and unyielding rock, she brought joy, even plastic flowers, to soften the edges.

She was Britain's only professional female climber, but more importantly, a devoted mother to Tom (6) and Kate (4). On 13th August 1995, she and seven others were lost to an avalanche on K2. The mountains claimed her, but not her spirit. I still carry a plastic flower on every climb, because Alison believed that even in the wildest places, beauty belongs.

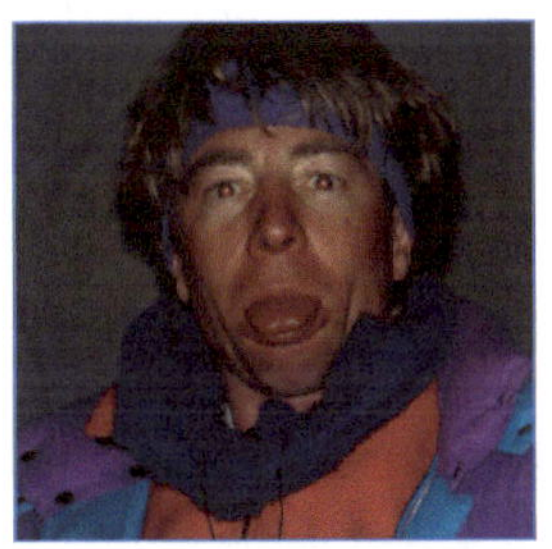

Rob Parker (35)

Rob didn't just explore, he redefined what was possible. He was a pioneer, pushing the limits of deep cave diving, spending days submerged in underground labyrinths where no human had ever been. He experimented with flooding his lungs with oxygen, stayed for a week in deep systems in Mexico, and was one of the few called upon to recover lost divers.

His stories of near-death escapes, of what happens when things go wrong, mesmerized me. He chased the unknown with a fearless passion, taking risks most couldn't fathom. In 1997, the depths finally took him. But every time I dive, I feel him there, a quiet guide, reminding me that true exploration comes with both courage and respect for the unknown.

Babu Chiri Sherpa (35)

Babu Chiri wasn't just a climber; he was a quiet guardian. At 22, the youngest on the expedition, I felt his watchful presence. He had climbed Everest more times than I could fathom, yet he still took the time to guide, to encourage, to believe.

His steady voice backed me when I set my sights on the summit. His belief became my own. His loss was a shock, a legend gone, a void left behind. But Babu didn't just climb; he lifted others. The Sherpa community, the climbing world, and those of us who knew him still walk in his footsteps.

Ang Rita Sherpa (72)

Ang Rita was the heartbeat of our expedition, a wiry, unshakable force of nature. With countless Everest summits, he carried a quiet authority, leading not just with skill but with warmth. At Base Camp, he taught me the little things, how to move efficiently, how to stay strong, how to laugh even when everything felt hard.

He trained younger Sherpas with the same patience, shaping them into true professionals. Whether setting up camp or offering a quiet word of encouragement, he was always the first to help. His wisdom, his humour, his steady presence, these are the things that stay with me. His legacy isn't just in the mountains, but in the people he uplifted along the way.

Introduction

"We've got to go! Now!" I yelled.

Pat, my friend and climbing partner, was less than a metre away. He couldn't hear me. The noise of the wind was too great. We were the only people on the mountain. Just the way we liked it. Everyone had headed down before the storm hit, except us. Now, after two days and nights trapped in the tent, the storm had us pinned down and escape was slipping further out of reach.

The thin nylon tent shell was blown flat across my body, forced down by the strength of the storm. I was on the windward side where the full might of the 150- to 200-kilometre-plus-per-hour winds were striking. For the last ten hours, I had been watching a small seam in the tent open and close with the tempo of the wind. The split had widened, shifting open and closed by one to two centimetres, on the verge of giving way. We both knew that the moment it did, our fragile sense of safety would vanish in an instant.

A few days earlier we were heading up for our summit attempt, but a climber higher up had been in trouble. Pat and I waited in our tent, melting snow and filling water bottles so the team ahead of us could quickly refuel and move faster down to the more oxygen-rich air below.

When the team passed, it was too late to leave for Camp 3. We decided to rest for one more night to head up early the following day. That's when the wind hit. It came out of nowhere. Not building slowly, no warning, just one minute calm and the next a roaring jet engine, like a bullet train passing at full speed. The noise was immense. The impact was immediate.

"That's strong!" I yelled to Pat. I had heard about the jet stream winds that raced across the Tibetan plateau and smashed into the high altitudes of Everest, but up until this point, it was just stories and distant clouds on hilltops. "What's it like outside?"

Pat tried to unzip the tent but the fabric was so tight that he could only manage to squeeze his head out of the bottom. There was room for just one tent at this camp. It was anchored with pitons and rocks and had an additional rope mesh lashing it onto the mountain even further. This wasn't going to be enough. The ridge was a few metres wide with thousand-metre drop-offs on either side. Some larger, waist-high rocks provided a little bit of shelter but still the tent stood proud to the ridgeline.

We shone our headtorches outside but couldn't see a thing. There was no sign of the wind. No spindrift dancing around, just a massive noise as this body of air moved around the world.

All that night, the following day, and into the next, the wind pinned us down. The tent shuddered and groaned under the relentless assault, holding on against impossible odds. We knew it wouldn't last forever, and when it finally gave in, we couldn't afford to be inside.

"Let's go!" Pat yelled.

Pat squeezed himself between the taut sun bleached yellow fabric and the ground. Then he was out and I was still inside. For a moment everything seemed silent and still. This shelter, made of nylon and aluminium no longer felt like home, it felt foreign. Somehow with Pat leaving everything seemed soulless, dead. As I glanced around, these objects that had kept us alive and comforted us for so long were now just that, objects. Time to leave. I slithered out of the small opening. Tried to kneel up but instantly my suit billowed up like a yachts spinnaker and I was blown flat on my face, pinned to the ground by an all-consuming invisible force. A sliver of Pat's down suit stuck out from the edge of a small waist-high boulder a few metres downhill. I wriggled and writhed my way inelegantly over the rocks toward Pat. This was now our only shelter.

Then, suddenly, it happened. Seams burst, thin aluminium poles bent like twigs, and before I could reach Pat, the tent exploded behind me. The wind tore through it like a knife, shredding the fabric in an instant. We had left just in time. Seconds later, and we'd have been wrapped in the wreckage, dragged off the mountain like so many before us. Now, there was no choice. We had to downclimb 1,500 vertical metres through the storm and reach safety before nightfall.

26th May 1995 : The night before the final summit bid

10:00 am. Leaving Camp 2b – 7,900 metres

We spent the night before camped at 7,900 metres. The cold bit hard. There were six of us in two tents, crammed in with three more people camped at Camp 2a, a snow ledge 300 metres below us. It was blowing a gale. Most of the evening was spent brewing up and trying to get as much fluid inside us as possible.

We had received a radio call at around 6:00 pm saying that our team in Camp 3 had counted the oxygen, ten bottles total, most partly used. Assuming two bottles per person per summit bid, there wasn't enough for the nine of us. Just four, maximum five people, would be going up. We had to make a decision there and then: who would go up and who would go down.

All of us deserved a shot at the top. We had each spent months putting up the route, ferrying supplies between the camps and preparing for this moment. Now, less than 1,000 metres from the summit, we needed to decide.

Of the nine of us, three had some type of sickness. Kelly had a badly injured knee, Mick had heavy bronchitis, Graham had a possible fractured rib and heavy bronchitis. Pat, Niama[1] and I were feeling good. Mike, Dorji and Brigitte were in Camp 2a, the ledge below us. None of us had climbed directly with them but as far as we knew they were all fit and healthy.

This was a really tough conversation.

Petitions were made, arguments put forth. The decision was made. Three of us, Kelly, Graham and Mick, would turn back while the remaining six continued up.

Pat, Niama and I left at 10:00 am that morning and headed through the rocks to Camp 3 at 8,235 metres. We deliberately set off late as we

---

1 Niama was an experienced high altitude sherpa and part of Russell Brice's Himex team. He had paired up with our team on his way up to support Russell and his team at Camp 3.

wanted to be up in the death zone[2] for the shortest possible time. Our plan was to be up above 8,000 metres just long enough to sort out gear, brew a few litres of water and then leave for the summit later that night.

The clouds showed that the monsoon front was approaching and the clear weather that we were experiencing was soon going to end. We needed at least one more night and a full day to get to the top and back. At this stage it looked touch and go if the weather would remain stable for long enough, but we went up anyway.

2:00 pm. Camp 3 – 8,235 metres

We arrived at Camp 3 exhausted. Niama had paired with Dorji and headed off at first light and were already here. At the same time, Brigitte and Mike moved up from 7,600 metres.

I reached camp around ten minutes before Pat and found Andre alone in the tent. He had come back down early that morning from his summit bid. Andre was teary, clearly physically shattered and lethargic and not really with it. Surrounding him was a sea of oxygen bottles. At least four of these bottles were connected to regulators. These regulators were emptying oxygen at their full flow rate freely into the tent. He had created a kind of oxygen-rich seal and had been sitting in this oxygen saturated environment for most of the day.

Andre was determined not to let either of us into the tent. He yelled and fought to keep his little oxygen enriched sanctuary intact. We were well into the death zone now and Andre was clearly suffering a delusion of safety brought on by fatigue and the relative warmth of the sun on the tent, yet unless he got down lower in the next few hours it was likely he would be in serious trouble.

Eventually Pat and I unzipped the door and slid inside. While Pat distracted him, I managed to turn off the bottles one at a time. Andre said that he had had a minor heart attack on top of the Yellow Band and had come down, luckily alive. He now couldn't bring himself to pack up and move to the lower camps, so he had just waited in the tent. After over an hour of discussions and sly distractions, he packed up his belongings and headed down to Camp 2a at 7,600 metres.

---

2 The death zone is a region of the Earth where there is not enough oxygen for humans to live. In other words, the body consumes oxygen faster than it's able to replenish it. On mountains, this zone refers to regions above 8,000 metres. The exact level will vary by a few hundred metres depending upon atmospheric pressure systems at the time. It is believed that humans can survive in the death zone for sixteen to twenty hours before noticeable deterioration of the brain and body functions occurs. This could result in loss of consciousness or death.

The tent was basically empty besides a dozen oxygen bottles all in various states of open. We now had to go through all the bottles to see which ones still contained oxygen. Most were empty, the rest near empty. None were full. We stacked the empty bottles outside the tent. Back inside, we went through and arranged all the other bottles in piles of level of their fullness. Four bottles were over half full, with the remaining six about a third full. Our summit strategy of taking two full bottles per climber wasn't possible anymore. We needed a rethink.

We checked the regulators and connections to ensure everything worked. At about 4:30 pm, Brigitte and Mike arrived. They looked really tired and headed past us to the two higher tents where Niama, Dorji and Russell's[3] team were. Russell was in his tent with one of his climbers, Mikko. He was waiting in support for three climbers from his team who were attempting the summit that day.

We had radio contact between the tents. Just talking, let alone moving, was hard at this altitude. Pat and I settled into our routine of melting snow and filling water bottles. Even to move, to think about moving, took so long. Lifting your hand to your mouth felt like it would take thirty seconds. Even thinking about breathing would take time. It was crazy, there was no oxygen up there. We were at 8,235 metres, higher than virtually every mountain in the world, and we were going to camp. The air temperature was around –20°C. Fortunately, for the moment, there wasn't much wind. With clear skies, we were looking good for the next day.

The radio crackled and Mike and Brigitte asked if we had checked their oxygen. We told them that we had been through all of the remaining cylinders and there was less oxygen left than we thought. They said they were too tired to collect their bottles now, so they'd do that at 11:00 pm before we left.

"Not a great idea. Better to get it sorted now?" we said.

A pause. They must have been discussing what to do. "No, not now. We're too exhausted."

So we waited, melted snow and brewed a lot of liquid.

---

3 Russell Brice, from New Zealand, was the owner of the climbing expedition company Himex. Our expeditions had paired up at Base Camp to support each other in leading the route and setting up the camps on the mountain. Russell had a small team of climbers who were also making their summit attempt over those two days.

6:00 pm. Bob returns from the summit. Camp 3 – 8,235 metres

Just after sunset, Bob arrived back at high camp. He was so exhausted that he just fell on the tent. Pat and I quickly opened the zip and pulled him inside. He looked finished.

"Don't do it. Don't go!" he pleaded. "It's much harder than I imagined. It's deadly. Don't go up." Bob's eyes were wide, and I can remember how scary his face looked.

We removed Bob's crampons and made him hot drink after hot drink. As Bob regained his strength, he recalled the story of his climb to the summit. Seven of them had left. Four from our team, Bob, Lama, Patrick, Andre, and three from Russell's team, Greg Child, Karsang Namgyal and Lupsang Temba. Andre had turned back lower down. The others proceeded together to the final summit ridge. The ice was rock hard. Lama was in the lead cutting steps, Bob behind him, and Patrick, Greg, Karsang and Lupsang behind.

"Lama was tired," Bob said. "He'd been cutting steps with his axe and I thought I'd take over. We weren't far off the top, maybe ten to fifteen metres. I don't know what I was thinking. I was right behind him, so I just stepped out beside him and whoosh, I was gone. The ice was so hard that my crampons didn't grip the ice. They just slid over the surface. I fell head over feet. All I remember was building up speed and not being able to stop. I tried to arrest my fall but my axe wouldn't stick to the ice. I hit the rocks and flipped over. I don't know how but I ended up face down, my chest on a rock, watching my cap falling down the 6,000-foot[4] drop. Rocks and snow kept falling over me. I just hung on and watched everything falling down. I couldn't move. I was so scared. It took ages but the others managed to get a rope to me. I had to let go of the rock and hold onto that rope. That was hard. Finally, I stood up and cut steps to the top. You got to be careful up there. That's a scary mountain. I nearly died today."

7:00 pm. Radio call. Camp 3 – 8,235 metres

A radio call came through at 7:00 pm. Jon was on the other end calling from Advanced Base Camp. "Now that there's less oxygen available, we decided that only four of you can continue up. Two will have to remain behind."

Pat and I looked at each other. Regardless of what they said, we

---

4 Approximately 1,800 metres.

knew we were heading up together with or without oxygen. Then the radio came back to life.

"Dorji and Niama, you will remain behind in support with one of the fuller bottles of oxygen just in case something goes wrong."

Brigitte and Mike were on the radio from their tent. Brigitte was wanting to delay leaving until dawn when the sun would make the route warmer. We discussed this, but besides her, all of us wanted to leave that night. We felt we weren't going to sleep much anyway so we may as well leave at 11:00 pm. This plan gave us the most time possible to get to the summit before the jet stream winds hit the top, which was typically around 9:30 to 10:30 am.

9:00 pm. Camp 3 – 8,235 metres

The tent was pitched on a steep angle. With the three of us plus gear and oxygen, it was cramped and uncomfortable. As soon as the sun went down, the temperature started to plummet. Bob was exhausted and weak, understandably bruised and sore, but relieved to be alive. He kept muttering, telling us how dangerous it was and how much harder he thought the climb was than expected. We kept melting snow and giving him more fluid, and he kept telling us about the route.

"It's much harder than I thought it was going to be," and, "You've got to be careful. It's really scary. The technical rock climb is infinitely more challenging than anything before."

That was when I started to think, what have I let myself in for? But, you know, up until then, I'd been able to handle it.

Pat and I were quiet and after a while, I wasn't listening to Bob anymore. As he spoke my mind drifted off to images of the mountain and what lay ahead. I just wanted to get on with the climb.

The wind had started its evening roar. You could hear it blowing against the thin tent, trying to tear us from our ledge and deposit us in the glaciers way below.

Then it got cold, freezing cold. Pat and Bob were in their sleeping bags, I wasn't. I had arranged with Andre that he could use my sleeping bag lower down the mountain and I would use his up here. Without carrying the weight of my sleeping bag, I was able to carry more supplies up to Camp 3. Unfortunately, when Andre had eventually headed down the mountain, despite a lot of protest, he had insisted on packing his sleeping bag and taking it with him. This had left me without a sleeping bag. I only had the clothes that I had climbed in to keep warm. As night fell and the temperature dropped, I began to get really cold. I was clenching my teeth hard to stop them chattering and my body was shivering like a leaf in the wind, nothing violent just a constant motion back and forth that I couldn't stop. At this stage I had no idea that I would be up above 8,000 metres without a sleeping bag for the next two nights.

Around 10:00 pm, the last of our cooking gas ran out. The familiar background roar of the stove was replaced by the cold wind outside. Within seconds the mountain's icy embrace had found its way into the tent once again. I could feel my skin tightening with the cold around my face, yet if I didn't move, I could somehow control my shivering.

Then the wind started to grow stronger and angrier. There was nothing we could do but lie in the dark and listen to the mountain. I huddled up in the middle. Bob was on my left and Pat was on my right. I lay down, put my arms around my chest, and closed my eyes, trying to get some rest, but I couldn't. I could shut my eyes, but that was about it.

10:40 pm. Inside the tent. Camp 3 – 8,235 metres

I looked at my watch. 10:40 pm. Twenty minutes to go. Nearly time to leave the comfort of the tent and step out into the howling wind outside. Would we be able to stand up in the wind let alone climb? Only getting outside would tell us. But it was so cold.

I checked the thermometer on my backpack. It showed –30°C inside the tent. I was about to step into the coldest, most dangerous night of my life.

10:55 pm. Radio call. Camp 3 – 8,235 metres

Just before 11:00 pm the radio broke the silence.

"Hey, guys. You still good to go?" Mike asked.

Neither Pat nor I had expected to hear Mike. For the last month or so we had been climbing mostly alone. The two of us were a team, moving up and down the mountain on our rotation. We had spent our time between pushing out the route, carrying loads to higher camps, or resting lower down. We spoke to others as we passed them or rested at the camps. 6:00 pm was the only regular call we received.

Pat looked at me and smiled. I gave a thumbs up. "We'll see you at eleven."

"Have you got our oxygen?" Mike asked.

"We've got four bottles, two for each of you but they aren't full," Pat replied.

We were using a relatively new Russian Poisk oxygen system. Each bottle weighed roughly three kilograms, and at sea level, lasted six hours in "climbing" mode and eight to twelve hours in "off/sleep" mode. The reality was that with the low temperatures and pressures above 8,000 metres, those times were reduced by at least a third. Additionally, this type of bottle couldn't be easily closed. They had no true "off" position, only the "sleep" or "on" modes. This meant that once they were opened, the oxygen would constantly leak from the mask even when unused. To turn them off fully you needed a special tool, which took time and was difficult to use.

Pat and I attached our regulators to the first of our two bottles. Neither of mine were full. One read just below half, the other only a third. The minimum oxygen most people tended to take for the summit was two full bottles. The first to get to the Second Step and back, the other to get from the Second Step to the summit and back. With less than one full bottle in total I knew that even with both bottles, I barely had enough to get to the Second Step. Still, the mask across my face kept me warm and I wanted something just in case I needed it. I hadn't set out to climb Everest with or without oxygen, but I knew I'd prefer to have it on me than not have anything at all.

I connected the one third-full bottle, turned the valve to the lowest "off/sleep" position, and slid the second fuller bottle beside it into my backpack. My logic was that it would be better to have more oxygen on the second part of the climb higher up.

My headtorch was on. I went through my gear one last time.

"Hey, is it okay if Mikko tags along with your team?" That was Russell, the leader of the only other team up there. Mikko was Finnish and didn't speak much English.

"Sure," Pat replied.

11:00 pm. Ready to set off. Camp 3 – 8,235 metres

I unzipped the tent door. The loose fabric flapped wildly in the wind. The cold immediately enveloped me. My sinuses snapped frozen, and what felt like lumps of ice formed inside each nostril. The water in my eyes froze and I had to keep blinking to unfreeze them. It was like having a scratch on the eye that you couldn't fix.

I remember the instant blast of cold air rushing into my mouth. The cold froze all the moisture around my lips, gums and tongue. Freezing air rushed down, deep into the core of my body. Each breath burned my throat as I inhaled. My lungs felt like they were being torn apart, frozen on a full inhale. For a moment, they remained this way, frozen, my body seemingly forgetting a lifetime of training on the simple act of breathing. In a panic, my brain registered the static motion of my lungs. When it remembered what to do, my body overcompensated by crushing my lungs and then immediately gasping for a new breath, at which point the entire process started again. It was a similar feeling to when you've dived underwater for too long and come to the surface gasping for air. The same thing was happening to me now. Burning cold air in, hold, a sudden gasp of air and more burning. It was only by physically concentrating on my breath that I was able to get my lungs under control, but nothing I did could stop the burning cold from penetrating every inch outside and inside my body. I had to work hard just to warm the air from –30ºC to body temperature with every breath.

Pat and I were packed up and ready to go. We'd gone through the oxygen and equipment. That's when I looked at this ten-gram headtorch bulb. I remember looking at it and thinking, *it weighs too much*. It could have saved my life later. I'd gone through absolutely everything to cut down the weight, at least twice, but I had last-minute worries.

Handling the metal ends of the oxygen bottles had frozen my fingers and they were now next to useless. I laid the crampons out. Attached the front, snapped down the back. Clipped the safety strap around my ankle, stood up, kicked my boots together to check they didn't fall off. They remained on. Good. Pat was doing the same.

Brigitte and Mike walked down to our tent. They looked tired. Generally at this time of night, you start to sleep. We'd all already done a hard day of climbing that morning and the days before. Pat and I had hardly slept from the North Col two days earlier, and I imagined Brigitte and Mike were the same. They had decided to do their final summit push differently from us. To maximise their time resting in the relatively higher oxygen at lower altitude and minimise their time up high, they had gone for a much faster and longer final ascent. They had covered a longer distance in a day less than us. Their summit ascent started in Base Camp, a night in Advance Base Camp, a night at Camp 2a at 7,600 metres, then Camp 3 and through to the summit. Pat and I were exhausted from being stuck up high in the storm at 7,900 metres the week before. So, when we made it back down to Advanced Base Camp, we decided to save our energy and rest there for a day, then do a slower ascent: one day to the North Col at 7,000 metres, the next to 7,900 metres, then here to Camp 3, rest, and summit. With only a few people ever having been up this high on this side of the mountain, no one really had any idea what the best strategy was.

Brigitte wasn't feeling comfortable with the amount of oxygen she had. She dropped her pack and frantically started going through her gear. Neither Pat nor I had climbed with her before, but we knew that she was an experienced climber. She and her husband Jon (Muir) had kept fairly much apart from the rest of the expedition. Jon got pulmonary oedema a few weeks earlier and could no longer continue. So, Brigitte had changed partners a week earlier to Mike. Brigitte was still cursing to herself and insisting on finding more oxygen so Pat and I methodically went through all the bottles again.

Tonight, the summit winds had arrived earlier than usual and they were already getting stronger. The monsoon storms were about to engulf Everest either today or tomorrow. When they did, the climbing season would be over. All of us knew this but none of us wanted to say anything. We were already out of cooking fuel and soon oxygen. Besides heading down, the only option was to keep heading up. Tonight was the night to climb or not at all.

Pat looked at Brigitte and Mike and said, "These are what's left of the bottles and none are full. You have the last of it."

Mike was calm. He just wanted to get on with the climb. Brigitte wasn't happy and wanted more oxygen so she headed back up to Russell's tent. I took the spanner and turned on my oxygen. What had read three out of seven bars during the day suddenly read one and a half bars. It didn't matter now. I'd head up and see how far I got.

Mikko was at Russell's tent getting ready. He hadn't got involved in the last-minute oxygen issue and had already set off up the mountain. We wasted over thirty minutes waiting for Brigitte to sort out her gear and were now all cold and anxious to get moving. There were no other climbers on any other route on any side of Everest. Only fourteen people were left here on the North Side: the five of us heading up, the six who climbed yesterday who were heading down, plus the three waiting at Camp 3. It was time for us to go.

Summit Day : 27th May 1995

The temperature had fallen even further, probably around –40 to –50°C plus wind chill. My eyes were exposed to the air. Each time I blinked hard, my eyeballs unfroze, then a second or so later they would freeze up again. It was a weird feeling, not overly painful. Like having some grit in your eye that no matter how hard you try you just can't remove. You blink, the eye clears but almost instantly it refreezes, causing the gritty sensation so you blink again. You try rubbing it away with your mitted gloves but that doesn't work. Like the frozen lungs and frozen sinuses that you are also dealing with, you surrender to knowing that this is just the way it is. The grit isn't shifting. Besides, you have bigger issues to deal with than a pair of frozen eyeballs.

There was no moon. It was completely pitch black apart from the light cast from our headtorches.

Brigitte hadn't reappeared from Russell's tent, so we assumed that she had decided to try a faster ascent at dawn that she proposed earlier. Mike led off first, then Pat and me. About one hundred metres from the tents, I noticed that one of my crampons was loose and about to fall off. It hadn't happened before but, in the cold, the two springs holding the back of the crampon had frozen open. I stopped, banged my ice axe against the crampon, breaking the ice off around the spring then reattached it to the boot. By the time I had done this I had dropped fifty or so metres behind the other two.

After about fifteen minutes I caught up with what I thought was Pat halfway up the face of the Yellow Band. He was moving really slowly. It was in fact Mikko, not Pat. His right crampon was hanging off his boot, attached only by the safety strap, but he hadn't yet noticed it. It was just being dragged along.

I said, "Mikko, your crampon's undone." I shook him and this blank face just looked at me. "Mikko," I repeated. "Your crampon's undone."

He stopped to sort it out. He didn't want any help. When I turned around, I saw Brigitte leaving the tents and heading up.

My body felt warm now that I was moving. I felt good. I felt strong. I soon caught up with Pat and Mike.

At around 12:30 am, we came to this enormous snowbank. We had to decide whether to go along the snowbank or up the face. If we missed the correct route through the Yellow Band, the delay would probably mean that our summit bid would be over. Eventually, we decided to climb up the snowbank to a small gully and from there find our way up through the rocks.

I remember the wind blowing hard and feeling very exposed. Luckily, we were climbing at night and couldn't see the huge drop below. We climbed with big plastic boots, crampons, and bulky gear all on these very loose rocks. It wasn't a good place to be. I remember feeling that the difficulty of the climb had gone up massively from the previous few days.

The slope steepened. Rocks bounced down the face as we climbed higher. A natural, safe distance developed between us to avoid getting hit. We kept moving to keep warm. Whenever I paused for a rest, the cold crept into my jacket and around my face. My focus was to get to the top of the Yellow Band, up to the ridge.

Mike and Pat had stopped at one of the gullies below the Yellow Band.

"It looked obvious from below but now I can't see which is the right one," Mike said. "I think it's this one."

Mike began to climb up, Pat behind him. I hadn't yet started climbing up before Mike yelled, "This isn't it. You can't get through the top."

"I'll keep heading up the slope and see if I can find the gully," I yelled.

The problem was dozens of little interlocking gullies fingering down the face. The line through these rivers of rock and ice looked straightforward when viewed from a distance. Now that we were on the route in the dark, gazing up at these near-vertical gullies, finding the correct line was proving difficult.

I found a gully that looked to link through to the rocks above. It was about six metres wide at the entrance where I stood and narrowed at the top. My headtorch wasn't strong enough to see the exit but it felt right. I began climbing, digging in my ice axe and kicking my crampon points into the rock and ice.

A few metres on I saw the frayed end of a white rope. It was only about two centimetres long, protruding from the ice. Someone had been here before.

"Over here," I called out to Pat. "I think this is the one."

The gully split into two and I went left. Pat followed. Mike came up behind.

"Wait," Mike called out. "It's this way, to the right. I'll go up, you follow."

I was relieved as the gully I was climbing got steeper and the rock looser. Pat and I downclimbed and then followed up behind Mike. We could see Mikko and then Brigitte moving up the slope above the tents. They would catch up to us while we worked out the route through the maze of gullies.

12:50 am. Through the Yellow Band – 8,400 metres

I reached Pat but we didn't talk. He waited for Mike to finish climbing, then continued up the next section. This next gully was shorter, only four to five metres in height, but a lot rockier. Loose rocks, mainly small hand-sized chips, bounced down the face. Every so often, a much larger plate-sized boulder bounced past. The rocks were hard, sharp and angular. We weren't wearing helmets.

I peered around the edge of the rock that I was sheltering behind to see how close Pat was to exiting the gully. Nearly there. My headtorch formed a narrow beam in the gully. With the sparkle of ice particles mixed with rock fragments, it looked like car headlights shining down a road on a rainy night.

I looked back and saw that Brigitte had passed Mikko. They were making their way up the first small gully towards me. Pat had cleared the short climb, and it was now my turn. I moved onto the steep rock and immediately felt the difference. The rock was loose and the ice cover thin and crumbly. My crampons struggled for purchase. What if the crampon released again? It was around this point that my mind and body began to feel like two separate entities, not combined. My body was the machine and my mind controlled that machine. I gently balanced the tips of my crampons on finger-sized rock ledges. All the pressure was on the front points of my crampons. *Oh, God. Why, after all the months of climbing, did my crampon come off today?*

I delicately, slowly, made my way up, starting on the left where there was more ice, then carefully moved right over the looser broken rock, scraping my crampons at the surface of the rock and ice for purchase on any ledge. Rocks fell down, pitter-pattering between my legs. I exited and saw Pat waiting for me. He looked focused. We were a team, but I knew that today, he was concentrating on the top.

We were on a good ledge and from here, we could see the entire ridgeline with the summit silhouetted against the night sky.

"That's it," Pat said, pointing to the summit. "One step at a time." His World War II cone-style oxygen mask covered his face but I could see from his eyes that he was smiling.

1:30 am. Separation in the Yellow Band – 8,450 metres

I hadn't realised it, but Mike had carried up a third bottle of oxygen. He must have taken it from Russell's tent before coming down to ours. That bottle was now empty. He stopped, changed over to another then continued up the gully.

Bits of loose rock and ice were falling as Mike climbed so Pat and I waited away from the fall line until he was clear of the gully. Pat went up next.

Brigitte caught up to me. She asked, "Why don't you go up?"

More rocks were falling so I told her I thought it was too dangerous to climb with all the rocks but she could go ahead if she liked. She decided to wait. I turned back to check the gully. Pat had reached the top, traversed right and was now out of sight. Mikko had caught up and was now behind Brigitte. I stepped into the gully and continued up. This was the last time any of us saw either Brigitte or Mikko that night.

1:45 am. Gullies towards the First Step – 8,450 metres

The gully was a scramble. I reached the top expecting to see Pat but he wasn't there. There was no moonlight. It was pitch black. This ledge was more exposed. The wind had picked up and the chill numbed my face. Ahead and above me was a maze of rocks. Pat and Mike must have continued up towards the First Step. I couldn't see them or their lights but that didn't matter. I just had to keep going.

Now outside the protection of the rock and ice gullies, the wind made the cold even more intense. My headtorch began to dim. I stopped and tried to adjust it. The headtorch was the old-style Petzl with a big battery at the back. I tapped it, shook my head, and tapped the front, but nothing. The battery must have been losing power in the cold, causing the light to dim. I could barely see the ground ahead. The light went dim, then black. Pitch darkness. I tapped the front. It turned on again but very dimly. It was way too cold and windy to try to fix anything. I let my eyes adjust to the night sky. I thought about the battery and bulb I had left in the tent. It didn't matter. It was so cold it would have been impossible to change them in these temperatures without getting frostbite. There was little moonlight but still there was enough light for me to see a few metres in front. I kept moving upward.

3:00 am. Waiting at the First Step – 8,500 metres

I arrived at the base of the First Step around 3:00 am. The wind had picked up strength and swirled around the rock face. This section was a few metres of climbing up a mix of rock and ice. It didn't look technically challenging, but I needed to focus to avoid making any stupid mistakes.

That's where I met up with Mike and Pat for the first time since the gullies of the Yellow Band. The last hour and a half I had been climbing by myself. I felt relieved to have caught up with them. We had agreed that 3:00 am would be our first radio call and the plan was to do this from either the bottom or top of the First Step. Mike had set a good pace and we were on time. We made the radio call. Jon asked about Brigitte. Brigitte had spoken to Base Camp about her plan to leave at dawn and not climb through the night. We agreed that Mikko and Brigitte were together and if anything had happened that they were close enough to get back to camp. We spoke about waiting at the top of the First Step for them, but it was clear that would be hard. The wind had picked up and it was much stronger up on the ridge, and this night was exceptionally cold. Mike and Pat had been there a few minutes longer than me and were getting cold. We decided that we should keep climbing, but I said I would wait back for five minutes at the top of the First Step to see if I could see any lights from their headtorches.

Mike moved on up the rock and ice climbed first, then Pat and finally me. The climb looked straightforward enough. Head straight up the snow and ice, then traverse across to the rock and exit onto a ledge that steepened to a cliff. Pat was now at the top, shining his torch down the route. My headtorch still played up but the wind had cleared the clouds and the stars helped highlight the route. I crunched my crampons in and sunk the shaft of my axe into the crunchy ice. It was good ice. Not too hard, not too soft.

Kick, kick, axe, kick, kick, axe, rest count for ten. Kick, kick, axe, kick, kick, axe, rest count for ten.

Heading up the face took more out of me than I thought. Soon my rests for ten weren't enough. Counting to fifteen helped, yet I was gasping for air. It didn't matter how deeply I breathed, I still couldn't get enough air into my body. I remember seeing my friend Alison Hargreaves powering her way up the long snow slope to 7,600 metres from the North Col. She would do thirty steps before a rest. She was strong. I could barely manage twenty steps in a row at that altitude and now I was down to only a few before resting.

I got to the top and got blasted by stronger wind. Now on the ridge there was no shelter. I reached Pat. "Gee. It's hard to breathe," I said.

Pat smiled. "Perhaps this ice isn't helping," Pat said, pointing to my oxygen face mask.

I reached up to the mask and realised that its entire front was one solid lump of ice. No wonder I found it hard to breathe. It was like running flat out but only being able to breathe through a straw. As soon as I broke the ice away, I gasped at the air. Wow. That felt good.

"It's too cold to wait here. Too exposed. They must have turned back. I'm going on. You coming?" Pat asked. He was right. The wind was stronger on the ridgeline. Climbing the face below had probably made me sweat. Now with stopping, I was losing heat fast and the sweat was freezing to my body.

"You go on. I'll wait here for five minutes and look out for them."

Pat nodded and moved off.

I kneeled to make my profile smaller and give myself some protection. I couldn't see any signs of anybody following. Within a few minutes, my feet began to ache. My fingers felt numb. The wind penetrated every seam of my suit, gloves and all around my face. I remember thinking I was getting frostbite, my fingers, my extremities, my nose. I remember how quickly I went from feeling cold at the bottom to extremely cold on the ridge. I had to keep moving. I waited for a few minutes longer but couldn't see any lights. I turned and continued up the route.

Step, step, step, rest for ten.

3:30 am. The rope to nowhere – 8,525 metres

I kept moving slowly up the slope until the ridge.

Step, step, step, rest for ten. Step, step, step, rest for ten.

Slow and steady. Slow and steady.

Step, step, step, rest for ten.

I couldn't see anyone in front of me so I wasn't surprised that I couldn't see anybody behind either. There were no ropes or signs that people had been here before. Over seventy years of climbing Everest, only a handful of people had ever made it this far.

The route weaved around various rocks and ice ledges below the ridge. I had to carefully shuffle from one ledge to the other with rocks, snow and ice tumbling off the huge drop directly beside me. The ground began to steepen, fast.

The wind was howling, I was cold, my brain felt numb. All I wanted to do was lie down and go to sleep. The only thing that kept me going was my focus on survival. If I stopped for ten to fifteen seconds, I immediately froze and it took ages to get warm again. I just had to keep moving up.

Out of nowhere, the frayed remains of a three-stranded white twisted rope appeared. *That's got to be a good sign,* I thought. *Rope means someone's been here before so I must be on a route of sorts.* It had been over half an hour since I had seen either Mike or Pat's headtorch. Doubts had crept into my mind about whether I should have traversed to my right earlier. I planned to keep going upwards, hoping to hit the ridgeline and follow it to the top. Now this old rope.

Step, step, step, rest for ten. Step, step, step, rest for ten.

After a couple of metres, the rope split into two. The left strand continued directly up, and the right, a metre or so in length, was half-buried, broken and frayed. I hadn't expected this. Do I head up towards the ridge or right along a cliff face with no apparent exit? I chose left, to the ridge and headed up.

Step, step, step, rest for ten. Step, step, rest for ten.

Five steps forward, the rope ended to the left of an ice-coated rock. I stood there, looking towards nothing but deep dark black. I looked to my left and it was the same: black. To my right, I could make out the outline of a half-story-or-so high rock face. Something didn't feel right. I stopped for about a minute, then another minute, getting colder and colder but just trying to work it out. Heading back down to the knot seemed like such a massive effort. The plan was to keep going forward and up but why was my body hesitant to take the next step?

Standing still with the wind coming in to my side, my core was getting colder. My body had long stopped shivering. I was tired and resigned to the cold. I don't like this. *Think, James. Think. Something just doesn't feel right.* I had trained for this situation. There were no specialised trainers or guidebooks on how to prepare for Everest so I made up my own. I blew up thirty balloons every day to help strengthen my lungs, climbed around 100 flights of stairs most days with a 25-kilogram pack, ran, swam, cycled and pumped iron at the gym. I knew a time would come when I was beyond physically exhausted, yet I would still need to make the right decision. Each day, after every prolonged exercise, I tried to train my mind to make logical, correct decisions while feeling completely fatigued. I answered crosswords and maths problems, memorised then repeated poetry, wrote sponsor letters and did anything I could to ensure that my brain kept working and didn't fall asleep while my heart was still racing.

So now, what was my brain, my senses telling me to do? Step forward? Climb up the rock? Head back down and traverse the face? If only I had light, then I could see. But I didn't. *Think, James.* I turned around, downclimbing to the knot. At least here I was safe, on the rock. Moving into complete darkness was unknown, whereas touching a rock was certainty.

It was much later, during daylight on the way down when I passed this same place, that I realised how lucky I had been. The frayed rope I had followed headed up to an old camp. Anchored on the rock face were the last remnants of what looked like a tent. Where I had been standing at the end of the rope was the Kangshung Face. A near-vertical two to three-kilometre drop. I had been standing unknowingly right on the edge of this face. Not even five centimetres further forward and I would have fallen. A single step would have seen me step off and tumble to the bottom. No one would have known how or where I died. I just would never have returned, put down as another mystery Everest fatality. Yet I didn't take that step. Instead, I felt something, maybe the lighter air density of the void, something not right and I turned around.

4:30 am. Alone towards the Second Step – 8,550 metres

It was pitch dark but I continued up along the narrow ridge. I could see nobody either in front nor behind. I was unroped. I was alone. I was freezing. The wind had increased and my headtorch was failing again. I just kept moving forward, making my way through the rock and ice, slowly upward.

Step, step, step, rest for ten. Step, step, step, rest for ten…

Around 4:00 am I began to see the first signs of dawn. The deep valleys and glaciers to my right were still pitch black, but the peaks of higher mountains were golden with the new day. I had made it through the night. Now it was time to survive the coldest part of the day, twilight. "Keep going, James," I kept saying to myself. "One step at a time."

I made it onto the ledge in the dark but saw Pat already climbing the ladder near the top of the Second Step. I just wanted to stop and rest for a bit and I'd been hoping to do this before having to climb up the next steep section. I had to catch up to Pat. I needed to keep myself moving, but big rocks fell off the cliff beside him so I had little choice. I grabbed a quick rest until he was over the Second Step.

The morning light also brought the reality of life. In the dark I was able to block out my fear of the exposure but now it was here. Before reaching the base of the Second Step I had to traverse a narrow rock ledge. The ledge was sheltered from the main wind but a constant cool updraft streamed from the glacier kilometres below.

I was directly over the mighty North Face. For weeks I had been looking at this photogenic face of steep rock and ice. I'd watched countless avalanches rampage down and seen it basked in glorious light as winds ravaged its crowning summit above. Now I was on it, nearing its top, looking directly down. I felt calm. Climbing alone for so many hours had made me feel at one with the mountain. Up until now, I had no fear, just appreciation. This was no ordinary mountain. She was magnificent, regal in a land of giants.

5:10 am. The traverse to the Second Step – 8,550 metres

Pat was nearing the top of the Second Step when I saw him next. Separating us was a narrow eight- to ten-metre steep traverse over thin, angled, flaky rock. A couple of old wind-battered fixed ropes were strung across the traverse, attached to the rock face by six weather-worn pitons. One piton at either end, two together in the middle, and another each side of the middle.

The traverse was exposed but looked easy. Clipping and unclipping takes time, and I just wanted to get across the section faster to catch up with the others. As it was, none of the pitons looked secure anyway. One of the challenges of climbing the North Side is that the rock bedding tilted down away from the slope, rather than into the mountain, meaning gravity slid the rocks down the face, not into the face. The freeze-thaw erosional effect quickly turned hard rock into loose rubble. The pitons had been hammered into one of the flaky cracks in the rock. The metal piton warms in the sun and then cools at night. Over the years this process is repeated again and again, thousands of times. This slight expansion and contraction movement loosens the pitons, making what was once a solid anchor wedged in a crack into a loose, wobbling unstable anchor. The North Side of Everest, especially above the Yellow Band, is just one cracked, loose rock sitting upon another. Constant rockfalls are therefore a part of climbing this side of the mountain.

I carefully moved onto the face and along the narrow ledge, trying not to look down. Concentrating on my foot placements, I reached the middle two pitons. They were hammered in about thirty centimetres apart. Then, I'm not sure what came over me. I didn't keep moving through this section. I stopped. I must have been hypoxic because I wondered how these pitons could stay in such a loose crack. How much weight could they hold? Would they be strong enough to support a fall? Perched on a cliff face many kilometres high, I did an idiotic thing. I tested the pitons' strength.

Balancing on the front of my crampons and letting my ice axe dangle from my wrist off its sling, I removed my hand from the rock face and held the rope. I pulled the rope one way then the other. The piton wobbled and twisted loosely in the crack. Then, pulling the rope slowly so it was now under tension, I watched as the piton became taut in the flaring gap. *That's good,* I thought. Then I messed up.

For some reason, I gave the rope that the piton was attached to a yank. As I did this, the piton "popped" and came out of the crack without resistance. I began falling backwards. I had pulled hard and fast on that piton, and it had, not surprisingly, given way. I was tipping back quickly and with no way of moving my feet to regain my balance, I was about to fall head over heels and cartwheel down the North Face.

Luck saved my life. As I fell backwards out of control, my left hand must have raised up and miraculously slid between the rock face and the rope. Rock fragments spat and tumbled around me but my arm held the rope. I could feel my heart thumping. My chest and ears boomed. Adrenaline rushed intoxicatingly through my body. That was too close. Why did I do that?

Then there it was, my first dead body, slumped on a ledge just ten metres below. It was at rest, like a piece of discarded rubbish, except for one thing. The more I looked, the more something about the person didn't seem right. One of its arms was missing, ripped off, with the strands of faded blue fabric flittering in the wind.

I felt empty, I couldn't absorb it all. I needed to keep my focus on the climb.

I gazed up to see Pat nearing the top of the face. He would never have known if I fell. One moment I'd have been there. The next, gone. I carefully hurried across the rest of the rock and got to the ledge below the Second Step. Pat was climbing over and into the warming sun above. Well done, Pat. Now it was my turn.

5:30 am. Base of the Second Step – 8,550 metres

The Second Step was in front of me, mostly rock with little snow cover. It was broken into two sections, a rock scramble of about two to three metres on the lower part, then a six- to eight-metre vertical rock face. A vertical crack stretched up the left of the face. This feature ran nearly the entire way up the face until it hit a small overhang and a large boulder at the top.

Besides this prominent crack, the rest of the face comprised more minor cracks and pock marks where chunks of rock had fallen out. Running up the left of the face and over the crack was a timeworn, bent and twisted aluminium ladder fixed to the rock over thirty-five years before by the first team to climb this part of the route, Chu Yi-Hua and Liu Lien-Man. On the right were old ropes in varying stages of decay. The sun, wind and ice had split all the ropes and created a massive knot about four metres above the base of the ladder.

I climbed up through a crack, traversed along the right and then around a big boulder until I arrived at the ladder's base. Just before the bottom of the ladder as I was coming up this last, technically difficult part of this small rock climb, I thought, *Gee, this is getting pretty hard.* I looked down and saw that my entire mask had iced up again. I snapped it away and looked at my oxygen flow rate. It was off. It was windy and cold, and I was alone and out of oxygen. I imagined that Pat and Mike would be waiting for me at the top of the Second Step. I wanted to get up quickly and join them, but I also knew that this is where most deaths occur on this route. With one slight loss of footing, one small mistake, I would fall off the cliff and it would be definite death.

I remember thinking, *Do I clip into the ladder, take off my back-pack, discharge my old oxygen bottle, attach a new one and put my pack back on?* I was too tired and I was too cold to stop. The sun was shining at the top of the Second Step but the rock face was still in the shadow. If I changed my bottle with my frozen hands now, the risk of me accidentally dropping the bottle or backpack was too high. I also thought the ladder would go all the way to the top. I could climb over into the sun and change my bottle there. How wrong I was.

5:40 am. The ladder. Second Step – 8,570 metres

The ladder was about six to eight metres long. It was connected by two very loose, skinny bits of cord attached to two piton anchors, one at the base and one two-thirds up. These two pitons shifted in their cracks left and right each time the ladder moved in the wind.

The bottom piton was no longer fixed firmly to the rock face but moved wildly in its crack, ready to pop out at any moment. The rope connected to the ladder was equally weather-worn.

Years of storms had bent, twisted and dented the aluminium ladder so it no longer stood straight. Its two legs were no longer in alignment and only one rested on a small, sloping ledge. The other was bent about ten to twenty degrees off centre and barely touched the rock.

Some very old, weather-beaten fixed ropes were dangling down to the right. I should have checked them more thoroughly, but I didn't and I made another mistake. All I wanted to do was to get to the top and into the sun so I could change my oxygen. I connected my ascender to one of the less worn pieces of rope and continued up. These ropes were so frayed from the strong winds that constantly smacked them against the rock that their external protective sheaths had been destroyed and only the inside straggly bits of rope coiled around each other were left.

I carefully stepped on the ladder. Immediately it pivoted outward and swung around on the solitary leg, then tilted back over the huge vertical drop behind me. Every time I shifted my weight the entire ladder swung. The right ladder leg, which barely connected, now hung loose in the air. It seemed incredible that this ladder had survived with all the years of storms up there, but I couldn't imagine it would last much longer.[5]

---

5 Pat told me later that when he ascended the ladder it was more securely attached. He said that there was a third piton that fastened the top of the ladder to the rock, making it vertical and stable. It must have detached after he stepped off, releasing the rockfall that I saw. I was the last person to ever touch that ladder. The following year it was not there. Put up in 1960, 35 years before, it had eventually blown off during one of the many storms that ravage the mountain.

I moved back off the ladder, stood on the little rock shelf and looked up. I wanted to free climb the wall. The problem was that the obvious rock line ran directly in the crack behind the ladder. I reluctantly and gently stood back on the first rung.

One rung at a time, I continued slowly and carefully upward without rest until I got to the second piton. Every movement, no matter how slight, swung and rotated the ladder left, right and back. The wobbling piton was anchored only a centimetre or so into the thinnest flake of rock and tied off with an old thin cord by a bowline to a rung in front of me. The ends of the cord had frayed so much that the worn bit was now the locking part of the knot. In no other circumstances would I have trusted my life to any of this, but here I was and this was Everest.

About two-thirds of the way up the face, I hit the massive knotted bits of old rope. I'd thought I'd selected a rope that missed this knot. I hadn't. My ascender wouldn't go any further; it was caught in the mess of knots. I had to get the ascender off the rope and either climb on unattached or find a rope that was free to the top and reattach the ascender to that rope. I was stuck.

Pat's head suddenly appeared over the top of the cliff. "You okay?" he yelled.

"No!" I yelled, but his head disappeared and never reappeared. Shit. He wasn't coming back. Maybe he thought I said "Go!" not "No!" [6]

My heart sank. I had no oxygen and I was freezing, exhausted and drained. I just wanted to clip onto the ladder and rest but a voice inside me kept telling me to keep going because the longer I didn't move, the more likely I would freeze to death. I probably held onto that ladder for a minute. When I went to move the ascender, I found it completely frozen to the rope.

I tried to unfreeze the mechanism, but I couldn't fix it with my windshell mitten-style glove. I reached for my figure 8 descender from my harness and used it as a hammer to hit the ascender. The ice still wouldn't break. My core body temperature was dropping. I desperately wanted to go to sleep. I kept nodding off and having to wake myself up.

The only option was to take the windshell glove off my right hand, leaving two pairs of fingered gloves underneath. Using my index

---

6 Pat had been waiting for me at the top of the second step. It was even windier up there and cold. He thought he heard me say "go" and had to make a decision. Mike was already moving on up ahead to the Third Step. He made the right decision to continue moving up the mountain and support Mike.

and middle fingers, I thought that I just may be able to better work the mechanism and break the ice inside the ascender. I wiggled the ascender for a couple of seconds. That failed. I needed more force. I hooked my elbow around the ladder and grabbed the ascender with my left hand. Now I could jigger the ascender with both hands at the same time.

I pulled hard and nothing happened.

I pulled hard again.

On the second pull, the ice shattered and the whole device came off the rope and disconnected. I had tugged so hard that I had nearly pulled myself off the ladder and the cliff face.

My left elbow unhooked from the ladder, my ascender came off the rope, and I started to fall back down this vertical cliff just like I had done below on the traverse. Yet again my left hand reached out to grab anything and amazingly, I caught a rope. I held on tightly then pulled myself back.

I didn't have time to catch my breath. I was freezing cold and I felt close to death. I put my wind shell back on and that was when I saw another body just below the cliff on a ledge, and then another, older, more weather-beaten body to its right and more old clothing and gear below.

5:50 am. Onto the rock. Second Step – 8,570 metres

The ladder was now angled beyond vertical, pivoting wildly left and right on its one leg. Besides the two thin ropes holding it to the rock face, that leg was the only piece of the ladder actually touching rock. I'd had enough of this piece of metal. I needed to get off before the whole thing fell down with me still attached. I'd never used fixed protection like this on a climb before; instead, I preferred to trust my own rock climbing ability. I should have just tried to free climb the face. I was angry for being slack and not believing in myself. For me, if I couldn't climb the face without a ladder, I shouldn't be climbing this route in the first place.

Getting off the ladder midway up the face and unclipping from the ropes wasn't going to be easy. There was a thin, finger-wide crack to my left. I stretched out and placed the front two points of my crampons on this. I gently put the blade of my ice axe into the vertical crack running up the left of the face and twisted it. It held with the torque. My right hand reached up to a flattish angled ledge and I pulled up. My hands were like clubs and I couldn't feel or grasp anything, but I could apply downward force.

The ladder swung as I transferred my weight from it onto the rock face. I don't remember how I got from that position up to the ledge. I must have pulled and scraped my way. I found myself crouching on the small, angled piece of rock under the overhang. I wasn't connected to any rope, but strangely, in this position, with my face pressed up against the rock, I felt relaxed. All I wanted to do was curl up into a ball and fall asleep. If I had just a short sleep, I'd feel better, I thought over and over again. I didn't want to look down. My eyes began to close and I slowly drifted off. As I did this, I rocked backwards ever so slightly. A shot of adrenaline rushed through my body and jolted me back into action.

I shuffled slightly right and threw my ice axe blindly onto the ledge above. I pulled on it slowly and gently as the claw edge scraped across the rock. Then it held. I just pulled myself over the lip. I remember thinking, *I don't care if I fall. I have just got to get up there. I have got to get into the sun. I have got to get warmth.* My axe had caught on the smallest of edges but had held. I slithered inelegantly over the top of the Second Step. My legs were still dangling over the edge. I shuffled the rest of my body forward and lay there. I was alive.

6:00 am. Warmth at last. The top of the Second Step – 8,577 metres

The top of the Second Step wasn't as flat as I'd imagined. I had to walk maybe five or ten metres before I was safe and in the sun. Although this wasn't far, I was so tired it still took a few minutes. Step, step, step, rest. It was then that I noticed that the entire front of my oxygen mask had once again frozen into a mass of ice. With no oxygen flowing, the moisture from my breath had filled and frozen the mask. No wonder it was difficult to breathe. I ripped off the mask and gasped down deep, lung-splitting breaths of air.

I knelt, opened my pack and replaced my empty oxygen bottle. The new bottle was just over a third full, still fuller than the first bottle but not enough to get to the summit and back. I thought, *James, you have got to get to the top and back down alive. More people die coming down the mountain than going up. You need oxygen to keep warm. You need oxygen to live.* So, like the first bottle, I turned it to the "off/sleep" 1 litre per minute position. My plan was to keep climbing upwards until I was too tired to go any further, then turn around and come back down. Throughout all my training I had never focused on the summit. Instead, I had consciously visualised coming down the mountain, returning alive. None of my friends back in Australia climbed big mountains and most Australians knew nothing about Everest except that it was high. Success for me was to return alive and to do that I needed to save as much oxygen as possible for coming down.

Ahead of me lay a snow ridge a few hundred metres long. Pat was already halfway along, walking really slowly but moving up, and Mike was approaching the Third Step. So much for the rest.

Step, step, step, rest for ten, step, step, step, rest for ten…

Step, step, rest for ten, step, step, rest for ten…

Step, rest for ten, step, rest for ten…

It was getting harder to regain my breath between steps. Come on, legs, move. Bend knee, that's it. Move weight forward, that's it, no, don't rest. No. Okay, rest just ten seconds, not more, just ten…. Now bend your other knee, pull forward, don't rest, okay rest but then keep going, don't stop the momentum…

My mind didn't feel connected to my body. The two were disconnected systems but joined in the way that a football coach isn't on the field but is still in communication with their players. I was simply giving instructions to a machine, my body, that had to keep moving. I felt mentally strong but my body was giving up. *Keep going, James. One step more. Then another. Don't overthink. Just keep moving forward.*

6:30 am. Snow ridge towards the Third Step – 8,600 metres

At this stage, I could see Pat and Mike at the bottom of the Third Step. Mike was already there and getting the radio out for another call. Pat was a few metres behind him. I had to catch up to them soon if I was going to make the top. They would get cold waiting for me to join.

I went up fast, too fast, as I forced non-existent thin air into my frozen lungs. Then, as I climbed towards them, my right crampon hit my left plastic safety buckle wrapped around my ankle and it exploded, breaking into pieces. The two ends of the strap fell loose around my ankle and became a trip hazard. If I tripped on this safety strap I would fall along the snow slope and into the rocks and over the cliff edge beyond. It would be tough to self-arrest there. Also, the broken safety strap was on the same foot as the crampon that had fallen off earlier this morning. Without a crampon, it would be impossible to make it down.

I could see the others ahead shivering and waving at me to come. So I continued, carefully considering every step I made on my left foot.

Step, rest for ten, step, step, rest for ten … keep going. You're getting there.

7:00 am. The Third Step – 8,690 metres

Eventually, I made it to the base of the Third Step and met up with Pat and Mike. This was the first time we had been together since the base of the First Step many hours before. I used a knife to cut off the safety strap. If the crampon came off again, then that was another problem to deal with. For now, at least, I wouldn't trip over it when I walked.

"Any sign of Mikko or Brigitte?" Mike asked.

"I waited at the top of the First Step but couldn't see them," I replied. "What do you think?"

"It was cold last night. Brigitte wanted to leave later when the sun rose. I reckon they turned back because of the cold," Mike said.

Pat was beside me, changing oxygen bottles and Mike was reclipping his bag. "You guys just switching now?" I asked.

"Yeah, I'm onto my last. I'm going to put it on 5 for this last bit," Mike said.[7]

Mike was a fighter. An ex-British armed forces paratrooper now working as a ski and mountain guide in France. "Solar powered sex machine," he would laugh as people ribbed him for being bald on top. He had a pale pink complexion, almost pasty, with incredible cheeky sparkling blue eyes. Whether in Kathmandu or halfway up a mountain he was always quick for a laugh and some banter. He carried a wiry strength, as much mental as physical. Despite being in the same team, we had largely been on opposite rotations up and down the mountain. Today was the first day we had actually climbed together over the twelve weeks.

Mike took the lead, Pat next, and me behind. Mike was powerful at this altitude, excelling and seemed to be very alert. He was a good person to have up the front. I had climbed most of Everest that evening alone and felt competent to keep going. I was, however, exhausted. I hadn't stopped moving since 3:00 am at the top of the First Step. I was freezing. The altitude was getting to me. I didn't have a headache;

---

7 The cylinder flow rate went from 1 litre per minute in the "off/sleep" position to 7 litres per minute in the "full" position. "5" refers to a flow rate of five litres per minute.

I was just exhausted and so very cold. All I wanted to do was sit down, rest and sleep. But they pushed on, so I pushed on too.

The small snow and ice climb of the Third Step was relatively easy. We moved to the right and over the top, heading onto the start of the long steepish snow slope. The slope was challenging but not so hard at this stage that we needed to cut steps in order to walk. That bit was still to come.

8:00 am. The endless summit pyramid – 8,750 metres

Mike had gone out fast and was halfway up the slope. Pat and I were catching up with him. I thought, *How is Mike moving so fast?* It wasn't long before he was forty metres ahead of me. Pat was close, about ten metres.

Step, step, rest for ten, step, rest for five, step, step, rest for ten, step… on it went.

Near the top of the snow slope we traversed right into a series of rocky gullies. We exited out of the rocks onto the final summit ridge. Below the summit along this ridge were a series of smaller ice ridges. Up, down, up, down, then finally up to the summit. Each ridge was about the size of a town-house rooftop but they were made up of windblown, super hard ice. I had never seen a mountain summit like this and was not mentally prepared for it. I had expected that the top of the world would stand proudly alone. Instead, it had a few mini-peak summits right before the top. Few people had ever made it to this point before and very few had written about or taken photos of this pre-summit feature. The top of the world was still a relatively unknown, undiscovered area. This was the exact spot where yesterday, Bob had slipped and nearly died.

Mike was cutting steps but I wasn't taking any chances. I was also recutting each step with my ice axe. Checking and rechecking each foot placement. *You got this, James. Just a little further.*

We reached the top of the rocks below the summit. Up until this point we had been sheltered from most of the stronger winds, but now, right below the summit, we began to feel its full force. The wind hit us. It was so strong that it nearly picked us up off our feet. We took shelter behind a rock until all three of us were together. We agreed to make a quick dash to the summit and then come back down and rest at this point again. We thought it would be too windy on the top for us to stay there for any length of time.

Pat was tired and slow. I don't know if it was because he was emotional from being up there or the lack of oxygen, but I remember thinking, *Come on Pat, we have got to keep going.* I overtook him on the rocks. I was now second behind Mike. I felt strong, as if I was at sea level. For the first time I imagined that reaching the summit was possible.

The top was close, maybe fifteen metres away. It was really there this time. I hadn't expected to feel emotional, but I did. This was the place people had spoken about, the highest spot in the world and we were about to reach it. A prominent, fairy floss-style cornice hung off the left side. It wasn't a flat summit; this was a definite sharp angular summit about the length of two table tennis tables. A lopsided one-metre-high aluminium tripod measuring device had been left on the top and this was covered in an array of prayer flags.

Nearly there.

Step, breathe for ten, cut, step, breathe for ten, cut, step…

Mike was in front of me. About three metres from the top, I stopped. Mike was just about there. Pat was a few metres behind me. This was Pat's mountain, not mine. This was his second time here. He had been my climbing partner for the last few months. He had chosen me over many others, the youngest and least experienced at high altitude. Pat was 37 years old and only a couple of weeks earlier I had turned 22. Together, we were the same age Mallory (37) and Irvine (22) were when they attempted to climb Everest and died on this same route back in 1924. We were a few steps off the top. I wouldn't have got this far if it wasn't for Pat's ever optimistic disposition and positive support throughout the expedition. This was Pat's moment.

I cut two steps to the side and waited. "Well done, Pat. Take us to the top," I said. I wasn't sure if he understood. He was already in his own mind. Memories and emotions were welling in his eyes. He looked at me and took three more steps to the summit. I followed behind and suddenly we were all together at the highest point on Earth.

9:15 am. Summit – 8,848.13 metres

Parents Finding Out About James Reaching the Top

James reached the top on Saturday, the 27th of May. Charles answered the telephone because it rang when we entered the house. A voice on the other end said, "This is Andy Broom from

Angela Allen (Mum) recalling the telephone call on 1st June 1995.

Coloured prayer flags flit across Nepal. You can see for miles. It's
incredibly beautiful. Like approaching a religious altar, the summit of
the world has a strong presence.

The wind had died down by the time we reached the top. We shook
hands, hugged and then sat down. Even thinking about what we would
do next took so much energy. I thought I was up there for five to ten
minutes maximum, but when we worked it out later, I must have been
at the summit for nearly three-quarters of an hour. It just shows how
slow my brain was working even though I felt okay. I had no sign of
altitude sickness and although I knew I was weak, I still felt internally
strong and confident I could make it down.

I had taken a Mexican sombrero to the summit because I wanted
to get a photo of it on top. When I initially got to Everest, everybody

was trying to do the first of something serious, so I thought, as a joke, I'd be the first person to wear a sombrero on the summit. I hadn't imagined anyone would care about me climbing this mountain, so I'd just climbed. Unfortunately, when I reached the top, I was too tired and forgot that I had the sombrero in my backpack. If I had opened my pack to check my oxygen, I would have seen it there, but the thought of having to undo two clips and do them up again was enough to stop me. I didn't want to check how much oxygen I had left, anyway. If I wasn't out already then it would be very close to finishing. When it ran out, it ran out.

I took off my face mask. I wanted to breathe the air undiluted at this altitude, leaving it off for the entire forty-five minutes I was on the summit. Also, the mask had iced up again, so it was easier to breathe with it off than on.

When I looked along the horizon, all the colour and definition within the atmosphere came through clear and sharp. The Himalayan range stretched as far as the eye could see from the east to the west. Looking out at the horizon, the Earth seemed to curve away, and to the south, we could make out the long black ominous band of monsoon cloud galloping towards us. There wouldn't be any more climbing for the season when that arrived.

The half a dozen or so 8,000-metre peaks dotted along the Himalayas stuck out like a giant would stick out from a forest of dwarfs. These giant peaks are enormous. Everest towers above all the massive 7,000-metre mountains, any one of which is higher than anything on any other continent. But Everest just overshadowed all these huge mountains. We could look across the glacier, see Base Camp and Advance Base Camp and see where we had come from the day before from Camp 3. It was terrific.

Pat pulled out the tricolour Irish flag. Mike and I did the same with our sponsor and nation flags. I hadn't expected to reach the summit, so back in Australia, I'd quickly bought a small, toothpick-sized Australian flag. While in the Rum Doodle pub in Kathmandu at the beginning of the expedition, I was drinking with some of the team. I got speaking with a group of Australian girls. "You've got to have a flag. A big flag, not that small thing. Here have ours. Just say our names on the summit when you get there." So, I pulled out their Australian flag and said their names and all the names of all my family and friends. At that moment, I reflected on all the people in my life who had helped, coached and supported me. I was there because of them. I was so grateful I burst into tears. I was now on top of the world, surrounded by my friends.

I was too caught up in my own emotions. I hadn't noticed that Pat had gone quiet. "I'm out of gas. I've got to head down," Pat said. I took one look at Pat and realised he wasn't well. His eyes and head were droopy; he had been slow on the final leg up to the summit, which wasn't like him and that was nearly an hour ago. He needed to get lower fast.

"Okay. We'll be right behind you," I said. That was at 9:45 am. I didn't realise things were about to get worse. Our day had only just begun.

9:45 am. Leaving the summit – 8,848.13 metres

My face was cold from the frozen tears. My body was starting to freeze up. It was time to head down.

Mike held the radio in his hand. His hat was off and his face was exposed. We had all removed our oxygen masks while on the summit. The constrictive, iced-up masks had got to all of us. The only difference I felt was the warmth from having something over my face. Since the sun was out, I didn't need the mask to keep my face warm. I hadn't really spent much time looking at Mike. I was too absorbed in my own little world. Now that I was standing, I noticed Mike wasn't responding. He wasn't well. He just sat there, slumped over.

I lifted my backpack. "Time to go," I said.

Mike's head was floppy and his entire body seemed limp. The radio was still in his glove but he wasn't life-like. I knelt and looked him in the eyes.

"Hey, Mike. You okay?" I asked. "Mike?"

Red and white drool hung from his mouth and his eyes looked like he'd had an all-night session in an Amsterdam drug den. He didn't respond, just sat there staring down the slope at nothing in particular. I took the radio from his hand, put it in his top pocket and zipped up his suit.

He looked directly at me and slurred, "I'm not good, James. I need to lie down." So that's exactly what he did. He just collapsed on his side and closed his eyes.

"Mike, you can't sleep here. You've got this. We're going down." I helped him sit back upright. Our faces were beside each other and we looked into each other's eyes. His oxygen mask was dangling loosely around his neck.

"You need to put this on," I said.

"I'm out of gas. All gone," he slurred.

"Here, Mike. Breathe some of this." I slid the mask straps over my head and pressed the cone-shaped cloth bag to Mike's face. His eyes opened, but his body was still lifeless.

"Mike, Mike, we're going to have to leave. We've been up here too long."

He rose slowly. We had left our tent eleven hours earlier. It was 10:00 am.

By the time we set off, Pat had disappeared from view. "The sign of a good climber," Pat once said to me, "is not how fast you can climb up a mountain but how fast you can get down." Pat was a good climber. Now I was alone with a zoned-out Mike, leaving the summit.

We took two steps and Mike collapsed again. "Mike, breathe this. I need you to stand." He looked me straight in the eye. He was exhausted and weak but there was a passion, a fight in the eye. He wasn't gone.

"Mike. I've got you. I'll cut the steps. You just follow exactly in my footsteps. Don't slip on the ice. Concentrate. One step at a time."

I was exhausted too. I'd had little oxygen myself and I was cold, and my body felt like a mush of jelly. Nevertheless, my mind was still alert.

"Okay, take one more breath and we're going. See that rock? That's our target." The first rock outcrop was ten to fifteen metres below the summit. A solid piece of light grey and green rock. It was just above the first trough of the summit ridge ice waves. At the base of the rock there were three gas cylinders. It was possible that they may have some oxygen left inside them.

Step, breathe for ten. Step, breathe for ten. Step, breathe for ten.

Step by step, we inched closer to the rock. It seemed to take ages, maybe ten minutes to cover the few metres, and eventually we reached its base. Mike collapsed in a heap. A bit of frozen drool hung from the corner of his mouth. I took my mask off and put it on his face. His eyes were closed as he fell onto his side, motionless.

Mike had the spare regulator and bottle-opening spanner in his bag. I reached over, unclipped the top of his backpack and pulled it out. My fingers were useless. Frozen lumps of flesh. I'd known they were cold for a while now but I didn't want to look. They had been cold all night but I hadn't managed to feel them at all since the Second Step. There was nothing I could do about it. I removed my Gore-Tex over-mitten and fixed the regulator to the cylinder. Turned it on, and … nothing. Again, on the next one … nothing. On the third … nothing.

"Wake up, Mike. Come on. Sit up!" I pushed him up against the rock. I was exhausted. I wanted to be back in the tents, not stuck here. He didn't have the energy to make it up the next ice slope and there was no way I could carry him. The only choice was to head straight down into the steep rocks below and traverse under the ice slopes, around the rock face, back to the snow slope.

How was I going to get him down this rock face? It was steep and rubbly. It ran for about fifteen to twenty-five metres before dropping off directly down the massive Great Couloir of the North Face. These must have been the rocks Bob had mentioned last night. One slip and we wouldn't be so lucky. With each step Everest seemed to peel away from below us. Rocks and rubble slid and bounced down the slope and off into the never-ending abyss below.

"Mike. I have to leave you while I find a way down. Okay?" I sat him upright against the rock, removed the mask from his face and put it back on mine. Then I stepped onto the rocks. We were a few metres directly below the summit.

10:25 am. The long drop – 8,835 metres

I got back to Mike, woke him up and pulled him to his feet. We slowly made it down the rocks. I was in front and Mike behind. He didn't look well. He was staggering, taking a long time to come down. What exactly was wrong with him? I knew he was struggling to breathe. We both were. I guessed he had pulmonary oedema but I didn't know much about cerebral oedema then.[8] He was solid and strong-minded. Being a paratrooper had probably trained him to focus on these things.

People will always ask me what my initial feeling was when I got to the top of Everest. Well, it's pretty funny, I hadn't been to the toilet for the last two to three days and all I could think about when I got up

---

8　High-altitude pulmonary oedema (HAPE) occurs when fluid accumulates in the lungs. At high altitudes, the reduced oxygen levels cause the blood vessels in the lungs to constrict, resulting in this fluid build-up. High-altitude cerebral oedema (HACE) is a critical condition characterised by brain swelling due to high altitude. Prompt recognition is crucial as it typically results in death within 24 hours if not treated.

there was having a poo on the top. Weirdly, at a dinner with the Tibetan mountaineering committee in Lhasa before we left, Greg Child said that he was creating a museum of things that have been to the top of Everest. Jon Muir put two chicken feet from his soup onto chopsticks and said, "I'll do the first chicken's foot ascent," and I said I had a sombrero. Greg said a frozen poo from the top would be funny. So, when I was on top, I was hit by this overpowering desire to do a poo. My whole brain was focused on going to the toilet but I didn't want to go to the bathroom on top of the world because it's a holy place. So I held it in. Then when Mike collapsed, I forgot about it, but now, just below the summit and directly above the Great Couloir on a dangerous traverse, I couldn't hold it in any longer. I needed to go. I looked at Mike. He was barely conscious.

"Mike, I've got to do a shit!" I yelled. "I can't hold on. Stay there."

Mike collapsed against a rock.

The urges were too much. Strangely, an old piton was anchored into this tiny ledge right in front of me. I put a sling through the piton and clipped in. I undid my drop seat on my down suit, squatted over the Great Couloir and let it fly. The wind was blowing hard up the slope and over the summit just above. As I let go, my last view of the summit was with my arse hanging off the side of the mountain. Not how I imagined I would remember the highest point in the world.

I went to pull my pants up and close my zips but the zips were too fine. My now frozen hands couldn't grip these small zippers no matter how hard I tried. Again, I told my body to keep moving. Keep awake. Keep alive.

Mike hadn't moved. He was still huddled over. His arms were hugging his chest. He was slumped sideways, resting against the rock. It was sheltered there, besides the breeze up the slope, sunny and warm. So easy just to drift off to sleep. His breathing was shallow and weak. He couldn't keep his eyes open for long and when they did open, they wandered everywhere.

"Come on, Mike. We've got to get down."

No response. His body looked like it was slowly shutting down. Nothing dramatic. No fits or spasms, just slowly curling up into a restful ball, similar to the bodies I had seen at the base of the Second Step. Was this what it was like to die? It seemed peaceful, not a bad way to go. Just a slow lack of breathing and the body shutting down.

"Come on, Mike. Wake up. Open your eyes. Look at me. That's it.

No. Keep your eyes open…" I took my oxygen mask off and held it to Mike's mouth.

"Hold the mask." But he couldn't lift his arms. "I'm not sitting down beside you. We're standing up. You got this. We've just got to get through these rocks. There are more bottles at the Third Step. We can check those."

"You go," Mike slurred. "I'll catch up. Leave me. Go."

His voice was weak but there was energy there somewhere.

"I'm not leaving the world's number one solar-powered sex machine up here. Breathe with me." My right hand held the mask over his face but I couldn't bend any of my fingers. I just had to push it into his face like holding something with the end of a stick.

I leaned into him, holding him close. The lack of oxygen, the physical support, the sun on my back. I closed my eyes and began to drift asleep, listening to his breath. The peace, the silence, was mesmerising. It felt strangely calm up here. An excellent place to sleep, just for a bit, just rest. Just a little sleep and I'll be fine…

We may have died if I'd sat down beside Mike, but I hadn't. Instead, I was standing facing him. I began to fall into the hypnotising trance of hypoxia too, rocking forward towards him. My crampons were resting on a thin ledge of rock and ice. As I swayed forward, the front points of my crampons began to move. This slow slip jolted me awake just as it had done at the top of the Second Step. My eyes opened. Shit, that was close. *I need to keep moving. We need to keep moving.*

Mike seemed to sense my sudden movement and his eyes opened.

"Let's get to the Third Step and we'll rest. Okay?" I didn't wait for his reply. I put my mask back on and pulled Mike up. Our eyes met and for the first time since the top, I saw a struggle for life deep inside him. He was fighting. We had a chance. We didn't say anything.

Below us was a steeply sloping rock and ice shoot. It fell away directly down the North Face. Everything was numb. The near falling asleep had frightened me.

I zig-zagged my way slowly through the steep rocks, trying to traverse back to the snow slope. Mike was just behind me; if he stumbled or collapsed he would fall into me and hopefully I would be able to catch him and stop his fall. He was fighting and moving. He knew the risks and what was at stake just as much as I did. The reality was I could barely hold myself up, so if he did fall, I doubt I would have been able to stop him. He probably would have just knocked me off balance and we would have both slid across the few metres of rock and ice and dropped off the cliff face together.

I wondered which was the rock Bob finally rested on when he fell from the ridge. There were two larger, body-sized rocks. Was it one of those? Or higher up? My mind was drifting, not concentrating on what was happening around me. I could feel it wandering. I knew I needed to concentrate but I was too tired, I just let it wander. It was the same feeling as driving a car when you're super tired. You concentrate, then concentrate on focusing, then forget what you're focused on and before you know it you're no longer in the moment but drifting off into another thought. I should have cared about Mike just above me but I didn't. I was in my bubble. If he fell, I'd have responded, but from a shock of adrenaline like before, not from some alert prediction of events. I was tired. So tired. Concentrate, James. One step at a time.

Step, step, breathe for ten. Step, step, breathe for ten.

We made it another twenty metres down. We were directly below the first rock that Mike had rested against earlier with the three empty cylinders. The summit was no longer visible. To me, this point, where you can no longer see the top, is when I disconnect from the up and connect with the down.

Both Ang Rita, our sardar, and Jon Muir had told me a similar thing at Base Camp: "Erect your tent slightly away from the main camp. Position it so you can't easily see the mountain. One of the difficult things about the North Side is your mind doesn't get any rest. For the next two months, you can never escape seeing Everest. You will hear and see people looking at her, don't. Base Camp is a place to rest and recover. Pretend the mountain isn't there." I was a complete novice at the big mountain climbs. The highest mountain I had ever climbed only took a few days, not months. Ang Rita and Jon were experienced and I lapped up their knowledge.

We rested at the edge of the rocks before the ice. Mike was coughing and dribbling and moving very slowly. Then, finally, he sat down again and he began to fall forward. I held him with my hand. I should have taken my mask off and given it to him but I was too weak. Too weak to do anything but concentrate on breathing.

Whenever I breathed out my body would forget how to breathe in again. It took all my concentration and energy to remember how to suck air in. So instead of a steady, slow, normal sea-level breath, I was breathing out, forgetting to breathe in, then suddenly struggling and gasping at a big deep breath in. That would be followed by a spate of fast, shallow breaths before I controlled my breathing again. Then I'd forget to concentrate on breathing in and the whole cycle would repeat. Such a simple action now dominated my entire consciousness.

We stayed there for what seemed like a moment but was probably more like five minutes. "Here, take this." I passed Mike the mask. He still couldn't lift his hands to hold it but that didn't matter. I pressed it across his face. I was getting annoyed at having to remove the mask all the time. It wasn't easy. The straps went over my head and it took an effort to pull them forward and over my goggles and balaclava. When I put it back on each time the frozen edges of the mask would twist and with my icy fists, I couldn't easily pull the flaps out to align the seal. By now, I would had preferred not to wear the mask. There was no oxygen and the claustrophobic feeling of breathing through an ice-choked-up mask was not good. Mike's mask was worse. It hung around his neck. The drool from his mouth had fallen onto the top of the mask and frozen. I broke off a big icicle drool, a mix of white stuff, saliva and blood.

"Two more breaths, then let's go. We're nearly there." I held the mask over Mike's face for a bit longer, then struggled with it again as I pulled it back over my head. I couldn't see Pat on the slope below so I assumed he was waiting for us beneath the rocks of the Third Step.

Mike was strong. Not weight room strong but mountain fit. He wasn't going to give up. He was a survivor. He was utterly exhausted but I knew that he wasn't ever going to give up while he still had something left inside him to give.

"Let's go. Let's rest at the base of the step and find you some gas." We stood up slowly and kept moving down. Very slow but down. Each step lower, the air got thicker with oxygen. The wind had picked up strength again and tiny snowflakes were swirling around. *That's good,* I thought. Stronger updrafts from below may bring up more oxygen-rich air from down in the valleys. I had no idea if this was true but the thought of it gave me strength. Anything helped now.

11:10 am. Towards the Third Step – 8,750 metres

The rock slope had taken a lot of what little energy and concentration Mike had left. He was starting to trip and stumble, falling over, sitting down all the time and just wanting to sleep, sleep, sleep.

Jon Tinker, who had climbed the same route in October 1993, said he experienced something similar on the way down. He told me how exhausted he was and just how much he had to focus on getting down alive. This route is perilous. It is steep, exposed, and long, with mixed rock and ice. Last year six people reached the top, three of them died coming down and another one had a near-death experience and was lucky to live. Up until this year, there was one death for every two people who reached the summit on this north side. Only fifty-six people had ever reached the top via the north and thirty had died in the process. Most people died slipping and falling off on the way down. So, with most of the descent still to go, the odds of all of us making it back alive were against us.

Mike's pulmonary oedema was getting worse. He was coughing up lots of blood and bile, spending longer unconscious than conscious. I found a little ledge to stop and then put the mask on him. He sucked on much of my remaining oxygen. I didn't care, he needed it more than I did. We then continued down through the rocks and ice gullies. I stopped at each discarded bottle and checked for any oxygen. Everything was empty.

It was just past 11:00 am. We had taken over an hour to get down the few hundred metres from the top. We needed to move faster. We were flirting dangerously with the Mother Goddess of Earth, Chomolungma. The high-altitude jet stream winds would generally have hit by now. We had been lucky. They were late today but they were coming and when they came, they just came, no warning. One second calm, the next, 200-plus kilometre an hour wind. We had to get below the Second Step before the winds hit if we were to have any chance of surviving. Below the Second Step, we'd be slightly off the main ridge and have a little more shelter. I began talking to my new deity, Chomolungma, "Please give us a few more hours to get down. Please."

Mike's skin was clammy and white. His eyes were droopy but open. "Mike, I'm going to check the bottles for gas." The regulator equipment we were using was old technology. It came directly from the bomber pilots of WWII. Likewise, the mask systems were ancient. Our cylinders were the latest lighter-weight fibreglass-wrapped Soviet Poisk oxygen bottles. The pipes connecting the cylinder to the masks and the seals would often break in the cold, rendering them useless. So we each carried spare bits of masks, pipes and connectors in our backpacks.

At the top of the Third Step, I clipped Mike into a rope. He just fell down the snow slope a few metres to the bottom of the face and collapsed. He didn't move. I was too tired to climb down. I connected to the old rope and controlled fast fell into the ice and snow beside Mike. I lay there motionless. I felt so comfortable and just wanted to sleep. I had fallen right beside Mike, who was luckily awake. It was now Mike's turn to help me. I was exhausted and just wanted to remain exactly where I was, but Mike encouraged me to wake up, and I did.

Beside me were four bottles. I checked them all: empty. Again, my fingers were getting colder and colder. I kept having to force my hands back into my wind shell. I just wanted to let them hang and dangle. I was so tired. Mike was getting worse. He was falling asleep and was now barely able to crawl. When he spoke, he was incomprehensible. His eyes kept rolling back, his head nodding from side to side. He was close to death.

Pat had quite rightly kept heading down toward the Second Step. There was nothing he could have done to help. Later, he said he had been feeling ill himself, so the best thing for him to do was get lower as fast as possible.

It was then, while kneeling to check the oxygen bottles, that I realised something was wrong with my arse and legs. They were cold, really cold, freezing. You usually don't feel your arse getting cold, but I could, and the back of my legs. I reached behind to find out what was happening. The drop-seat pants I had opened for my earlier crap were still open. My arse was exposed. For the last hour, with the wind blowing up the hill, I had had a sub-zero breeze blowing through my down suit and now, sitting on the snow, I could feel the cold. Only one layer of thermals lay between my skin and the snow.

As I checked the cylinders for oxygen and grappled with my cold arse, I had forgotten to check on Mike. I turned around and saw he was still sitting in the same position, with his eyes shut, but in one hand he held the radio. It was off, but if he had made a call to someone, I didn't know. Regardless, if he was strong enough to take out the radio and talk, he may be able to help me.

"Mike. I need your help."

He didn't respond. He slowly opened his eyes but stared ahead at nothing in particular.

"Mike." It was no use. He was still out of it and getting worse. "All these bottles are empty. We need to keep going."

Mike didn't move. Shit. My arse was cold. I had to close the hole in my suit. I tried twisting around and pulling it up. I managed a little but there was no way I could hold the zipper tight and close it. My fingers were all frozen rods, no longer capable of moving independently. My hand was a single stiff claw. We had been there too long.

I put the spare regulator inside my down jacket, took the radio off Mike, put it back in his pocket and zipped up his coat. I fixed my oxygen regulator on Mike again and let him breathe, but there was no sound and the dial read empty. I didn't have the energy to disconnect the bottle so I left it in my bag and left the mask hanging around my neck.

"Let's go." I looked at Mike. He had returned to a world of relative comfort and I could understand why. It was sheltered and warm where we were sitting. There was no freezing wind and the view across the Himalayas was beautiful. It felt the right thing to do just to rest a while, gain some strength and then head back down when we were strong enough. In front of us was a steady, few-hundred-metre-long snow slope. It headed directly to a collection of rocks, then down slightly to the left was the Second Step. That was our target.

I stood to go but Mike wouldn't move. Pat was now more than halfway down the snow slope. I needed to catch up to him and see if he could zip up my arse cover. The more I thought about it, the colder it seemed to get. I helped Mike to his feet. He stood hunched over but didn't move.

"We've got to go, Mike."

He looked at me and nodded. He didn't need my words. He knew what was required.

We walked, me in front, Mike behind, down the slope. I was exhausted but I didn't want to stop. We needed to keep moving. This was where my crampon strap broke on the way up. What if my crampon fell off again? I couldn't think about this now. We could stop at the top of the Second Step.

Step, step, rest for ten, step, step, rest for ten…

I could feel my arse getting colder, my legs were hurting and my feet were cold. I hadn't felt this before on the trip and I began talking to myself. "The back of my pants are open. What if my penis freezes off? What if I lose my penis?" The thought of losing some fingers or a hand was terrible, I could live with that, but being twenty-two without a penis?

Mike was moving but very slowly. We were now about halfway down the slope.

"Mike, I'm going to have to see if Pat can zip up my pants. I don't want to lose my penis."

Mike didn't register but he was still standing and still moving forward.

I turned to him. "I'm going down to Pat. I'll meet you at the Second Step where those bottles are. Okay?"

Mike didn't say anything but I knew he understood. He just needed to keep moving down, no matter how slowly.

I increased my pace. I needed to reach Pat before he headed down the Second Step.

Step, step, step, step, rest for ten.

Step, step, step, step, rest for ten.

Too fast. My lungs were burning. I was breathing so deeply I thought I'd explode but I was on a mission. Pat was almost at the spent oxygen cylinders. "Come on, keep going, James, don't rest. Think of your penis."

Step, step, rest for ten.

Step, step, step, rest for ten.

Step, rest for ten.

The faster pace had made my lungs burn with each rush of cold air. My nasal passages had been frozen since leaving the tent and my lips were cracked and bone dry but the burning cold air deep into my lungs hurt the most. I was now forty metres from Pat and I could see that he was focused on getting to the start of the next steep climb down.

Step, step, step, step, step, rest for fifteen…

11:55 am. Zip me up – 8,580 metres

We kept heading down towards Pat. Pat had also been without oxygen since the summit, so he was having trouble too. He searched for the half bottle of oxygen George, the only Russian on our team, had left at the top of the Second Step. Every time I sat down to check an oxygen bottle, snow and ice fell into my suit, which, mixed with the cold wind, meant my legs were getting badly frost nipped.

I caught up with Pat just in time, but the faster pace had made my lungs burn with each rush of cold air. My nasal passages had been frozen since leaving the tent and my lips were cracked and bone dry but the burning cold air deep into my lungs hurt the most. Pat fumbled with the zip, his numb fingers useless. He did, however, wrestle the flap into place, sparing a little more of my backside from the cold. Small victories on Everest.

I was frustrated with myself for not being better prepared and attaching my own pull tags on the suit. The down suit was a borrowed item, as was virtually all my gear. Ian Collins, a man who I had never met and who lived in Sydney, heard that I was climbing Everest. He had been on the south side of Everest in 1994 and very kindly sent me his down suit and high-altitude sleeping bag. Ian was a good ten centimetres shorter than me. The sleeping bag was okay but the suit was way too small. I didn't have the money to buy one myself, so I had no alternative but to use Ian's and adapt it. I'd cut the toe section off two pairs of thick socks and had one on each forearm and the other over my shins to cover the exposed gaps. The hood barely made it over my head and when I did put it on, it pulled the crotch up to insanely uncomfortable levels. Most of the time I put the hood down and wore a woollen hat. I knew from climbing in New Zealand that my hands usually became frozen claws in the cold, so I had attached longer bits of string to each zip so I could pull them with a cold, closed fist, except the one around my arse. My string had run out when I was doing this job back in Australia and I'd forgotten to get more and finish all the zips. I was now paying the price for that mistake.

On top of the Second Step, with my hands frozen, physically exhausted and the cold wind blowing up my arse, I had a moment of self-pity. What was I doing here climbing Everest? I was surrounded by my heroes. These were people who I'd read articles about in magazines and people who had written books about their trips. They were the real deal, and I was just a kid. Sure, I'd climbed many mountains but nothing compared to them. National Geographic was filming our expedition for an Everest documentary on the climbers and the new route we were establishing to the summit. They weren't filming me. They were there to film the famous climbers. I was just the kid that they were trying to give high-altitude climbing experience to. I was the one selected from all the others around the world, a real privilege, but really, what was I doing up here?

Mike had done well and was nearly down the snow slope. The wind was growing much stronger but we could still walk without being blown over. The sun was shining. We had been lucky with the weather, but Mike was slowing. Taking longer rests and shuffling. I should have headed back up the slope to help him but I was too concerned about fixing my suit.

Above the Second Step was a rubbish dump of spent oxygen cylinders all scattered around. Perhaps twenty in total. *One of these must have something left inside,* I thought. I knelt, took the spare regulator out, and began attaching, screwing, checking, removing, attaching, screwing, checking. Old frayed pieces of ropes and other rubbish were scattered about too. It was a mess. If one person had left a little bit of oxygen, I'd have something to give to Mike.

Mike made it to a boulder at the end of the bits of rubbish and collapsed. I finished checking the last couple of bottles around me. Nothing. All empty. I stood up, headed over to Mike, maybe four metres away, and sat down. His whole body was drained of energy and his head hung down. His eyes were closed and he was dozing in and out of consciousness. His breathing was shallow and he was wheezing.

"Come on, Mike, we are nearly there. Just get down this next bit and we're home," I said, shaking him.

No response. He sat rigid in the snow, the warm sun softening his frozen face. A single nudge and he would have toppled, left to rest where he fell. Three bottles lay scattered, one perched on the snow, the other two half-buried beneath shards of ice and tangled rope. I tried the first bottle, but nothing. The second bottle… shit! It had something. Very little, but something. I took the regulator off and tried the third bottle, again nothing. I reapplied the regulator to the second bottle, turned it on and handed the mask to Mike. "Breathe, Mike, there's some gas in this."

By now, Pat had located the partially full bottle George had left, connected it to his regulator and was heading to the top of the Second Step. I looked back at Mike. He breathed in deeply and his eyes opened. He managed nearly two breaths; on the second breath it was out. No hiss. The regulator level read zero. I shook the bottle. Nothing. I turned back to tell Pat. He was gone.

"That's it, Mike. There's no gas here. You need to get to the edge. We have to get down. Let's go."

We rose to our feet. Mike must have been feeling awful but he kept going, not giving up. If we could just get to the top of the cliff then we had a chance. Unfortunately, that was as far as our luck carried us.

I couldn't get him down myself. I didn't have a rope to lower him off the cliff. Every rope was knotted or broken pieces or both. I didn't have the strength to hold him, anyway. My arms and legs were frozen and my fingers were rigid. I could barely move any of them. I was exhausted. I wasn't going to leave him there. There must be a way. There's always a way. "Think, James. Just breathe and think." But I couldn't. The more I tried to work something out, the more the visions of the dead below came back into my mind.

What was I doing here?

It had taken us nearly three hours to move a few hundred metres or so downhill.

12:30 pm. Top of the Second Step – 8,577 metres

I looked down. The broken, twisted ladder now dangled at a weird angle to the cliff. The single piton midway up was still holding it in place but without it, it would have fallen backwards and down the face. The big knot of ropes was swaying and the rope tentacles flipped and twisted like a rampaging octopus. The wind had picked up to a steady, chilly breeze now. It was getting colder. The weather was changing for the worse, fast. We had been too high, too long.

No obvious clear rope ran from where we were perched down to the bottom of the ladder. Everything was being twisted and blown into the knot by the strong swirling winds. I couldn't see Pat. Had he fallen? Gone? I wouldn't have heard him. I didn't see him leave the top. *Shit, James, you're losing it. You should have watched Pat and seen what he did. He may have fallen and needed your help. Where is he?* I scoured the rock face below. Nothing. Down, down, down it went for thousands of metres. The bodies and parts of other bodies that I had seen at dawn dotted the rock ledges below. They no longer frightened or shocked me. They looked familiar and a natural part of the mountain view.

Mike was quiet again. The little bit of oxygen had worn off. He was kneeling, silent, eyes closed, perched right at the top of the cliff.

"Okay, Mike. I can't lower you down. You'll have to do this yourself," I yelled over the wind.

A half dozen or so bits of frayed twisted ropes hung off over the edge, all connected to a single aluminium anchor in a crack beside a large rock. I picked up each rope and flicked them. It was impossible to tell if they ended at the massive wind knot or went through to the bottom. Pat must have clipped into one of these ropes since he wasn't stuck in the knot. Three or so ropes hit the knot and the other two were blowing wildly around what appeared to be the outside of the tangle. They'd have to do.

"Mike, I am clipping your descender into this rope. You see it?" I threaded Mike's descender device into one of the ropes and back into his harness.

One eye slightly opened. He was still alive.

We got this, James. Just one step at a time, I said to myself.

"I'm going first. I need to be below to help you," I shouted. "If you fall, I'll catch you. If you get stuck in the knot, stay there and I'll come. But if you don't move when I call, I'll have to pull. And if I pull, you'll go over the edge. So move when I say. Don't make me drag you off the cliff. You're nearly there. Just hold on."

No response. Mike had drifted into another trance but that didn't matter, I was saying this more for my sake than his. I was frightened. I didn't know what I was doing. I was out of my depth and I couldn't make a mistake. I wasn't going to leave him. I just wanted to get down, home and off this mountain. I was a scared kid in the middle of nowhere with frozen hands, legs, arse and probably worse.

"Mike. When I call you, you come, okay? Just come. I've got you."

I attached my figure 8 to the other rope and fell into the abyss as inelegantly as I got over the lip all those hours before. I gradually went past the small overhanging cave and then whoosh! I fell. I had no strength left in my arm or grip to hold the rope. I dropped with such force and speed that it burnt a line across the Kevlar padding on my right hand glove. I don't remember the ladder passing me, the knot, or the cracks on the wall that I had used to climb up. I just shot past them all. My descender suddenly jammed with another rope about a metre up from the ladder's base. I was upright and swinging but I had made it. Shit. I made it!

I was a rag-doll on a string hanging from the rope down the bottom of the ladder. My descender had jammed in the mess of ropes. I was locked in. I needed to release the pressure from the rope and somehow unclip myself. "Come on, James. Keep moving. Concentrate on just one thing at a time." I bridged across with my right leg to a crack, and quickly placed my left leg on the angled wall. My ice axe dangled around my legs. I pulled that up with my left hand, held the blade on a thin ledge above me and pulled. Getting the weight off the rope enabled me to unclip the descender. I slowly let myself down and rested at the base of the ladder. I was down and amazingly still alive.

Something caught my eye to my left. Someone was coming around the blind lip before the rope traverse and it wasn't Pat. It was Niama. He was about thirty metres away, slowly traversing the rock face that separated us. I called out to him.

"Niama! Are you with Mikko? Brigitte?"

"No. Mike radioed. He needs oxygen. Jon sent Dorji and me. Dorji is behind."

Mike hadn't moved one bit from where I had left him. He was as still as a rock. Eyes closed. Kneeling. Arms across his chest. He was almost praying but he wasn't.

"Mike!. There is oxygen here. Come!" I yelled.

Nothing.

"Mike. Mike. Wake up!"

Nothing.

The thought of climbing back to the top filled me with fear. I didn't know if I had the strength to get back up that face. I needed to get him moving.

"Mike. Mike. Wake up. You need to come down! There's…" and like that, he rolled like a dead body forward and off the cliff.

He fell fast. The combination of both the rope around his harness and the way he tumbled forward meant he plunged headfirst. Luckily, a part of his body hit the massive rope knot. It flexed and tightened and nearly arrested his fall but he rolled left towards the ladder and then dropped again, ending face down in a mass of knots but slightly lower than where I was. He was unconscious or asleep but that didn't matter. He was alive and we were all down the Second Step.

1:20 pm. Base of the Second Step – 8,555 metres

I climbed over to Mike and released him from the tangle of knots. The ropes were a mess around his body, legs and arms but somehow, they had absorbed his fall. He was bleeding from the mouth and his breathing was raspy and uneven. He had most likely fractured a few ribs in the fall. Niama reached us and connected Mike into a new full bottle.

With the oxygen, Mike slowly regained enough energy to start moving. He moved down the final section of rock, extremely weak, he kept slumping and again drifting in and out of consciousness.

We made it to the fixed rope below the Second Step at the start of the traverse. I went across first; I didn't clip into the rope so I could move faster over the rock face. Pat was waiting on the other side.

Niama attached Mike to the rope. Separating us now was a fragile, exposed ledge, with the few kilometres drop-off directly down the North Face. The wind began to whip violently up the face. Clouds swirled around the ridge, and powerful blasts slammed into us as air surged up and down the near-vertical rock wall.

Very gently, Mike began the traverse. When he was halfway across, his legs just gave way and the inevitable happened. He began to slip then slide down the cliff. Niama was nearest to the far end and Pat was closest to our end. They both thrust their ice axes over the end piton and pushed down with all their weight, giving them more support in case the pitons popped out.

Mike slid chest down, feet down, for three or four metres. Rocks bounced and tumbled around him then fell silently over the colossal drop-off. His oxygen mask and sunglasses had been knocked off during the fall and when he looked up at us, his eyes were enormous. None of us said a word. We were all in shock. He had come to a rest a metre or so before the final edge. I could see the determination on his face. This was a do-or-die effort.

Gently and carefully, he moved his crampons onto a small ledge. He didn't need our help. He was alive and alert again. Blood pumping. The fall had given his body what he needed, an instant adrenaline shot. His eyes were still bulging, but he began to slowly climb back up the rock face. One foot, one step up. Slowly he hauled himself up.

He made it back to the thin ledge of the traverse line. He put one hand on the lip and onto snow. As he applied his weight, the snow gave way and the middle piton popped out. Again, he fell down the cliff but much faster and much further. Then another piton popped out. He slid further but with the added speed, he tumbled more than slid. Rocks scattered all around. Then he stopped. The rope held. He was right at the edge of the drop-off into the endless abyss of the North Face. Again, the rope arrested his fall. We thought he was dead for the second time in only a few minutes. The bodies and parts of other climbers who had died were around him. Stuck on the ledges. Climbers like us who hadn't been so fortunate and died right there.

"Mike!" we yelled, but he didn't say anything. It was clear he was in shock. I was too. He had survived another fall, just. This old rope and those loose pitons would only stay for a bit longer. He had to get the weight off the rope before they gave way.

For the second time Mike managed to climb up the rock face. When he came close, Pat helped him over to the snow ledge. Mike sat down and closed his eyes. Against all the odds he had made it. He was coughing blood, couldn't talk, hardly breathing, but the oxygen and his willpower were keeping him alive. We were together again as a team for the first time since the summit. The wind was increasing and the temperature dropping but we now had help and both Mike and Pat had oxygen.

I couldn't feel anything below the waist now. I was numb with cold. "Pat. Can you try and pull my pants up again?" I asked. Pat pulled and zipped as much as he could. I could immediately feel the warmth.

I had known for the last few hours that something wasn't right with my hands, especially my right one. Ever since touching the metal on the jumar on the way up, my right index and middle fingers didn't feel right. They felt solid. I removed the Gore-Tex shell, thick over glove and thin liner, and there it was. My fingers were frozen. Definite lighter discolouration of each fingertip ending abruptly in a white ring. I took a photo of my hand and put the gloves back on. There was nothing I could do about it up here besides keep going down.

2:15 pm. Down towards the First Step – 8,550 metres

"I'm going to keep moving," Pat said. "I'm not feeling great."

Pat headed down the ridge towards the First Step. Mike, Niama and I stood up and started to walk but at a much slower pace than Pat. Mike's breathing was gasping and heavy. He was crashing again. Struggling to stand up. Struggling to move. I was fading too. Tired, bone-tired, but still alert. The few hundred metres of vertical drop had given me a jolt of energy but I still had a long way to go. *Keep moving, James. Keep heading down.*

Step, step, rest for ten. Step, step, step, step, rest for ten.

Bit by bit, we inched down the slope. I'd attached a short rope to Mike in the hope of holding him if he happened to fall. After a bit I removed it. It was too dangerous. If Mike fell, I would never be able to hold him. I would be pulled off too. I decided that if he fell and survived, I would be there to help him. I was way too exhausted for anything heroic. I just wanted to get down.

Step, step, step, step, rest for ten. Step, step, step, rest for ten.

I turned around to check on Mike and Niama, thinking they were behind me. Shit, they weren't. Mike was sitting in the snow and Niama sat behind him.

"Okay?" I called back.

"Okay," Niama replied. "Resting."

"No rest. Keep moving. Don't sit down!" I yelled. "Mike, get up. Keep moving. Get to the First Step and rest. You have to move!"

The thought of heading back up the hill to him was crippling. Although Pat had zipped up most of my pants, I had now lost all sensation in my legs, and my arms were completely numb. Pat and I had had only a handful of hours of broken sleep during the previous few days of climbing and we hadn't eaten or drunk much either. All these factors, like cold, hunger and exhaustion, were compiling and catching up with me seemingly at the same time. If I wasn't careful, I was going to make a stupid mistake.

And that's exactly what I did.

I had been moving slowly with Mike and Niama. Pat was now down a few hundred metres ahead of us above the First Step with Dorji.

It had been pitch dark when I climbed this section of the route last night. The route down towards the top of the First Step was either to the right and up and over a small ridge, or straight ahead and along another rock face. The straight-ahead traverse looked narrow but not too difficult. The route to the right went slightly uphill. I decided to do the traverse since I couldn't face having to do even a small amount of uphill.

It all started well, slowly walking foot over foot over a series of holds about ten centimetres wide. The rock face had a number of disjointed offset ledges and cracks. To my left was the familiar near-vertical drop to the glacier kilometres below. I placed my crampons down carefully, walking almost in a forward direction and holding onto the face with my right hand, stepping down every so often. One ledge stopped and another ledge came into play. My hands worked along the rock. Soon, however, the ledges got thinner until I had to face forward onto the cliff. The ledges had narrowed so only the front points of my crampons would hold.

I had taken the wrong route. I hadn't done this on the way up. This was different. I was an idiot. I thought I had seen a direct, faster way down but it wasn't.

I was stuck on a technical move that I now needed to negotiate. I should have kept following the ridgeline as Mike and Niama were now doing. Going back up would be difficult and I didn't have the strength to retrace my steps along the cliff. Keep going down and I might just make it to a larger ledge then across and around. Why now? Why did I come this way? I cursed and felt sorry for myself.

"Okay, James. You got this. Work it out," I said out loud. "Keep going." I was balancing on the tips of my crampons. The handholds were good but my hands were following the rock bed sloping downward. Each time I grabbed a ledge it broke off in my hand. Applying downward pressure to the rock just broke the rock off the face and sent it tumbling between my feet and into the never-ending drop below. This wasn't a solid piece of rock but a series of millions of smaller broken rocks all piled up and glued together with ice and dirt.

I kept moving left and downhill, but the more I moved to my left and down, the closer my hands came to my feet. Soon, most of my weight was on my hands. I was shaking. I couldn't hold this much more and if I fell, there was nothing to stop me. I would slide onto the ice, down the next rock face and drop to the glacier floor below.

There was only one thing for it. About one metre below and to my left was a two-hand wide ledge big enough for just one of my feet. If I could jump down and across to that and hold onto the thin ledge above, I would be able to keep traversing off this cliff and over to the top of the First Step. The only big problem was I'd be landing on the crampon without the safety strap. The same crampon that came off in the morning. If my boot twisted on impact and the crampon fell off or I missed the ledge or hit the ledge but didn't manage to hold on…

"Let's go."

I jumped.

Landed. Rolled my left ankle and… *slice!* My right foot's crampon came down, penetrating the down suit up near my groin.

My left leg was perched on the thin ledge but was now spasming from the strain of holding my full body weight, but I couldn't move my right leg. I had survived the jump but skewered myself into a weird yoga position. I tried pushing the crampon down to make the rip bigger so I could manoeuvre it out of the hole but the suit wouldn't tear. I needed to work one arm under the right knee and help stretch and lift it. *Shit, James, why do you do this to yourself?*

Like the tension suddenly releasing from a rubber band, the crampon became free. I stretched my leg, bunny hopped onto my right leg and rested my left leg.

My heart was racing. *I want to go home.*

I made my way over to Dorji and laughed at how stupid I'd been. Pat was already down the First Step and heading towards the gullies above Camp 3. I waited for Mike and Niama to come down what was now the obvious, much simpler route. Mike was looking worse again; the oxygen boost and the jolt of adrenaline from his slip had lifted him briefly, but his energy was fading fast.

"I'll get down the Step and help in case he falls. Can you take him from the top?" I asked Niama.

I had never actually climbed with any of the Sherpas from the other teams. I'd seen them on the mountain, just as they'd seen me, but usually we were out front or passing each other while stocking the camps. I wasn't entirely sure of their capabilities, but I knew they were sensible and strong. The best thing I could do for Mike now was stay below him; if he fell, maybe I could slow him down or stop him, though I doubted I had the strength.

3:00 pm. Down the First Step and towards Camp 3 – 8,450 metres

Getting down the First Step proved more challenging for Mike. He was even slower now and finding it difficult to keep his balance. Three steps resting for ten seconds turned into two steps resting for twenty seconds. Half an hour later, Mike reached the bottom.

Dorji went ahead, Mike then Niama and I were behind. None of us spoke. We just kept moving. I could see Pat heading closer to the Camp 3 tents now.

We carefully worked our way down the gullies we had climbed earlier that morning. We passed the tiny piece of rope sticking out of the ice where I had seen Mikko pausing all those hours ago and I knew that we were safe.

The sun was setting to the west and the view looked magnificent. I sat on a rock and tears rolled down my face. A mixture of happiness, relief, sorrow and joy. I couldn't believe that I was there. How lucky and grateful I was for all the people who believed in me and helped make this happen. I was back alive and alone to watch a stunning sunset over the Himalayas as the massive, long shadows cast by the mountains crept into the valleys below.

It had taken nearly three hours to get Mike down from the First Step back to the camp. We had been going for over eighteen hours. With darkness falling, we wouldn't make it past Camp 3 tonight. I was resigned to another night at over 8,200 metres.

6:00 pm. The cold sleep. Camp 3 – 8,235 metres

We arrived back at Camp 3 on sunset. Russell was peering out of his tent towards us and motioned to put Mike in the tent with him. Dorji was already in that tent and Niama followed Mike in as well.

I continued walking down the hill to the lone single tent below. It was the tent that Pat, Bob and I had spent last night in. I didn't know who would be in there but I assumed at least Pat. I certainly didn't expect to find what I found. I reached the tent, removed my crampons and opened the door. It was empty. I didn't know it at the time but Pat, Brigitte, Niama, Dorji, Russell, Mike and Mikko were together in the two tents above. I was all alone.

I was too tired to do anything. The inside was basically empty besides a few used oxygen bottles and broken regulator gear. I would have to spend another night without a sleeping bag above 8,000 metres but I was too exhausted to care. I arranged the few bottles and other bits of rubbish as a poor insulation mat so I could lie on them rather than directly on the frozen rock below. I figured that the fibreglass wrapping around the bottles would probably give some insulation against the rising cold from the ground. I emptied my backpack and put my feet inside and pulled my arms into my chest. I remember thinking, *I don't care if I never wake up. I'm just too tired, too cold and too exhausted to do anything.* My arms, legs and fingers were frozen lumps. I was just so physically drained. All I wanted to do was sleep.

My fingers had already started to go black with frostbite. There was nothing I could do about that now, I'd just have to deal with that later. I could hear the wind and storm lashing the mountain outside. I didn't care. There were a lot of things that I should have been doing but I was just too tired. I drifted fast asleep.

5:00 am. Leaving Camp 3 – 8,235 metres

I woke before sunrise to the sound of Brigitte walking past my tent. Around 5:30 am Russell opened my tent flap. Over his shoulder I could see the first rays of light hitting the massive South Face of Changtse. I was still alive. Russell handed me a mug of hot water, my first drink in over twenty-four hours. He told me that Mike had nearly died multiple times during the night but he was still alive. It was time to pack up the tents and gear then head down.

The wind was already strong. The monsoon clouds that we had seen the day before rampaging their way northwards across Nepal were now hitting the south side of the mountain. Clouds billowed wildly up the rock gullies of the Yellow Band above and swirled aggressively on the summit ridge. The climbing season was over. We were now caught in a race to get down to the relative safety of the North Col and Advanced Base Camp before the big monsoon storms totally engulfed the mountain.

Mike seemed better than the day before but still in a poor state. He could at least stand but was unable to focus or communicate. Pat, Dorji and I filled our bags with rubbish and spare gear. We took it in turns to hold Mike and together headed toward Camp 2b. Mikko went down ahead by himself. Niama and Russell remained to pack up Camp 3 and then join us lower down. By 6:30 am the wind was already severe. We were the last people on Everest that season.

10:30 am. Down the mountain – 8,100 metres

Our packs were heavy but each step lower brought more oxygen and got us closer to home. We hadn't rested properly for days. We were exhausted. We had a long way to go that day and the weather was getting worse. Mike was moving but slowly, too slowly. We decided I would stay to help Mike while Pat and Dorji moved on ahead to pack up the tents and strip down Camp 2b.

Mike was delirious, in and out of consciousness, coughing and breathing hard. It hadn't taken too long before whatever drugs he had been given overnight wore off. He was drooling and couldn't verbally communicate or meet my eyes, but we knew we were together. There was only one objective and that was to get down as low as possible before the storm stopped us. We aimed to drop 2,000 vertical metres to Advanced Base Camp that day. I knew how quickly the wind built up and how strong it was from when I had been caught here in a storm just a few weeks before. With the monsoon hitting, every minute counted.

12:00 pm. Clearing the camps. Camp 2b – 7,900 metres

I reached Camp 2b exhausted. Helping Mike move downhill was hard. Dorji and Pat had melted some snow for us to drink. They had already gathered up most of the ropes and gear by the time we arrived.

I packed my sleeping bag, which I had left for Andre, and filled the remainder of my bag with group equipment to take back down the mountain.

I still hadn't eaten anything since we last ate here on the way up two days before, however, drinking was more of a priority than food. Little over a week before Pat and I had been stuck right here wondering if we would survive an earlier storm. That seemed like a lifetime ago. We were now at the start of another major storm but this time more tired and with much heavier packs to carry.

The next section down to Camp 2a wound its way through rocks. It was relatively sheltered, that wasn't on our mind. Looking down past Camp 2a we could see the big, exposed snow slope. Between Camp 2a and Camp 1 at the North Col was where the next danger lay: A few kilometres of snow slope connecting the North Col at 7,000 metres with the North Ridge at 7,600 metres. The ice-covered ridgeline was 100 or so metres wide and completely exposed.

Already we could see a large white plume of snow billowing off this lower ridgeline, a familiar sign that the winds were high. With nowhere to shelter, this section of the climb had already claimed many lives with climbers being either frozen to death or blown off its side into the glaciers below. Any other day there was no way we would contemplate crossing the slope, but with no food, little fuel and Mike ill we had few options other than to risk crossing the exposed slope.

Russell and Niama caught up with us at Camp 2b. We all saw what lay ahead. Niama and Dorji stayed to finish packing up the tents. Mike, Russell, Pat and I kept moving down to Camp 2a at 7,600 metres to clear that camp.

2:00 pm. Before the final slope. Camp 2a – 7,550 metres

We took a rest at Camp 2a and melted snow for a drink. Niama and Dorji joined us while we were pulling down the last of the tents.

Sitting in the snow at the top we looked down the next section. This was going to be hard. The wind screamed across the ice slope without mercy. A swirling, gusty cloud danced over the ridge like a torn tail of a kite snapping in the wind.

Mike and Niama had fixed the last section of safety line along the steeper part of the ridge early on in the expedition but this was no longer useable. The storms had battered the rope and popped the snow stakes and ice screws out of their holds. That rope was now a mess of twisted twine partly frozen to the ice and partly whipping like a stock whip in the wind. It was more of a liability than safety line. If we were blown off our feet or slipped, we would have to self-arrest quickly before sliding off the edge. This was a hard enough prospect early on in the expedition, now in our tired state carrying heavy packs, it would be near impossible.

Russell, Niama and Dorji left us at this point and headed down. Russell needed to get back to organise his expedition and thought with the speed the three of us were travelling that we would only make the next camp at the North Col that night before dark. To save time, Niama and Dorji could start clearing the North Col camp while we followed more slowly behind.

Pat was coughing hard and suffering from the effects of his pulmonary oedema. Mike was unconscious again, lying on the snow beside me. My index and middle finger on my right hand had turned black with frostbite so I couldn't grip anything, only use it as a frozen club.

3:00 pm. Snow slope between Camp 2a and the North Col – 7,300 metres

Pat went first, Mike, then me. Within a few minutes of leaving the camp we were being smashed by the strong wind. I don't know how Mike remained on his feet but he did. A problem was that the wind came in gusts, so one second you'd be leaning hard into it, then the next the invisible wall of wind wasn't there and you'd trip and stagger forward.

Step by step, inch by inch we progressed down. Pat was faster than both Mike and me and was halfway down the slope while Mike and I were still up high. When the wind got too strong, Mike and I held each other, huddling into the heaviest smallest surface area as possible. Neither of us spoke. The noise, ferocity and burning cold of the wind meant we were locked in our own battle of survival. I tried to hold Mike as much as I could but in reality, that wasn't much. There was no rope to save us now. One slip and it was over. I remember watching Mike leading up this slope early on in the expedition. A blue rope trailed out of his backpack as he slowly pushed out the route above. Mike had done a lot to establish our route on the mountain. He had put in more than most of us, carrying heavier loads, carving out the route and constructing the camps. I felt no weakness in my friend now coming down ill. He had given plenty to help others like me make the top, and so in my mind, and Pat's too, it didn't matter how long he took to come down. We were returning together.

5:30 pm. North Col to Advance Base Camp – 7,000 metres

The sun was setting and the big dark rocky face of Everest loomed above us. The first of the massive monsoon storms was settling on the summit ridge, battering the mountain, cleansing her of another layer of rock and covering her in her new icy coat. The door to the top of the world was definitely shut. We had made it out just in time.

Mike was now conscious and the most alert he had been since the summit. We were all hungry, thirsty and exhausted. The thought of spending another night on the mountain didn't appeal to any of us. We only had half a day's hike to go between us and the relative luxury of Advance Base Camp. A big snow face and then a hike over the glacier and we were there. We had been going for another twelve hours straight and still had a long way to go. It was getting dark but we decided to keep heading down.

Besides two tents, the North Col camp was dismantled. The crevasse between the tents was over half a metre wide. No one else was on the mountain. We moved through the camp quickly. The lower we could get Mike the better. His breathing was still erratic, he looked clammy and pastier than usual, and though his eyes were more alive, they still didn't look right. He needed a doctor, drugs and more comfort than we had here. Those things were all lower down.

The route down from the North Col to Advanced Base Camp was in bad condition. Everything had changed since heading up only a few days earlier. Some of the large overhanging ice seracs had avalanched off, removing most of the fixed lines that we had established below and making the route deep with rubbly soft wet snow and ice. The temperatures had increased and the snow was losing form. The fresh snowfall was avalanching around us but we weren't focused on that, we were heading into the thicker, oxygen-rich air below. There was no point clipping in to any of the few remaining safety ropes, speed was key. Pat and Niama were in front and Mike and I were coming behind. We had already dropped over one and a half kilometres in vertical height that day but Mike was getting tired. We were all getting tired.

Each time Mike sat down to rest, I found myself sitting down too. I wanted this to end but also strangely didn't. What did the future hold when I returned? I was here on the mountain with my friends. When

I got back things would be normal and no one would understand this strange high-altitude world I'd been in.

6:00 pm. Returning to normality. Advanced Base Camp – 6,400 metres

We made the base of the North Col at around 6:00 pm, right on sunset. Mike was looking better. We sat down and rested. At that point, we saw five people coming towards us. They came up with no backpacks, just flasks of hot tea and hot chocolate. We lost a lot of fluid up high and when we drank some hot tea, it immediately re-energised me. I felt like a new person.

We put Mike back on oxygen from the North Col. Halfway across the glacier this ran out and he seemed to go from okay to nearly dead in an instant. Someone radioed to Advanced Base Camp to send more oxygen. We tried to move Mike but he wouldn't move. His body was just physically exhausted.

After a while, someone came running up with an oxygen bottle. Unfortunately, this bottle was empty, so another person was sent up with a new canister. It was now getting late and much colder. Mike was in big trouble. Babu Chiri, the most experienced high-altitude climber of the time, tried slapping Mike on the face to wake him up but he was unconscious again. None of us had enough energy to carry him down. It looked like after all that we had endured, Mike was about to die so close to camp.

More people came up from Advance Base Camp to help carry Mike down. It took nearly two hours, but we eventually got back and laid him down in the mess tent.

We had reached camp well after dark. The wind was up and it was bitterly cold. The entire team came out to meet us. We had been lucky that year with thirty of us on the expedition and no one dead. This was unheard of for Everest's North side.

My Turkish friend Nasuh came rushing up with his big, bearded smile and outstretched arms. "My friend, you did it. I am so proud. You are the youngest Westerner ever to climb this harder side of Everest!" he proclaimed. "Everybody your age who has even gone above Camp 3 has died. You made it!"

"What?" I said. "What do you mean, died? Why?"

"Because your brain doesn't develop until your late twenties. The lack of oxygen kills younger people. You mean you didn't know this?" He laughed.

Why didn't anyone tell me this before I left? I had no idea. I was just climbing. Is being the youngest even a big deal?

Dick Price and Kelly Armitage, our doctors, got to work. Mike was unconscious again. They had him on full oxygen, intravenous saline drips, and injected him with drugs. Anything to keep him alive. When he deteriorated further, they placed him in the portable pressurised hyperbaric Gamow bag. It was working. He was coming around. Just conscious, but still alive.

I'd been soaking my frostbitten hand in warm water but now I was too tired to keep it there. Pat and I stayed up and waited with Mike until around 10:00 pm but eventually we collapsed into our tent. I crawled into my sleeping bag still in my summit clothes. I didn't get changed. I couldn't get changed.

The following day I went to see Mike. Dick and Kelly said that they thought he was going to die many times during the night, but he had made it through. His face was thin, his body was lean, he didn't have his regular smile, his eyes were dark and sunken in, and he looked close to death. But he had survived.

Epilogue

I never thought being the "youngest" to climb the North Ridge mattered. I did it because I wanted to, because I was invited. And who says no to Everest?

The sombrero was a joke, a nod to the ridiculous "firsts" people were claiming even back in 1995. I carried it all the way to the summit, only to forget to take it out of my backpack. No photo. No proof. Just a ridiculous story that still makes me laugh.

I arrived back in Australia thirteen days after standing on the summit. The doctors took one look at my frostbite, deep black spreading across my fingers and half my right palm, and immediately wanted to cut it off. That didn't sit well with me. Amputation seemed a bit drastic, I liked my hand. Instead, I decided to try something new, treating frostbite like a severe burn.

For months, I spent hours each day in an oxygen-rich hyperbaric chamber. Slowly, feeling crept back into my legs, feet, and arms. The last week was brutal, constant pins and needles, like electricity surging through my nerves. But it worked. My frostbitten hand healed at about a millimetre a week, except for the two stubborn fingertips on my right hand.

Six months later, one of my frostbitten fingers snapped clean off mid-game of squash. I picked it up, ready to play on, but my opponent, who happened to be the number-one-ranked player, took one look, turned pale, and forfeited on the spot. At least I finally had a way to beat him.

The other finger? That was a more hands-on job. I was tired of this dead weight hanging off my hand, it was getting in the way of climbing. So, I borrowed some pliers and got to work. A few stubborn tendons and nerves were still clinging on, and cutting through them sent a sharp jolt of pain up my arm. But once I twisted it free, that was it, just a bit of bleeding, which I patched up before calling it a day.

Those two fingers had pressed against the metal ascender on the Second Step, through two layers of gloves. The yellow rings I noticed in my summit photo, taken at the base of the Second Step, perfectly traced the frostbite's reach. Later, those rings made it into medical journals. Apparently, they were the highest recorded photo of high-altitude frostbite at the time. They even gave them a name, "Allen rings". I guess that's one way to leave your mark on Everest.

After the climb I spoke with Mikko about what happened to him on summit day. He told me that when Brigitte and he had met up with us in the Yellow Band they were both extremely cold. Brigitte had tried to convince him to return to Camp 3, warm up, and go again at sunrise. She descended but he chose to keep going up alone. When he reached the base of the Second Step, he decided it was too dangerous so he turned around and headed back down. When he reached Camp 3, he went inside a tent with Brigitte, Niama, Dorji and Russell. He told me that at sunrise Brigitte left to try her fast ascent but returned after an hour saying that she hadn't left enough time to make it to the summit and back that day. This was later confirmed with Russell when we met up a few years later.

Brigitte saw things differently. During a live television interview in Australia, the host asked her the obvious question: "Why did James, the less experienced climber, reach the summit when you didn't?" Her response caught me off guard. "My head torch failed. I tried to change the bulb and battery, but it still didn't work."

This was the first time I'd heard this. The idea of replacing a headlamp bulb in that brutal cold, without suffering frostbite, seemed impossible. But that wasn't the biggest shock. In her later books and public talks, she told a different version of events, claiming I had deliberately walked away, leaving her for dead. According to her, she was forced to bivouac at that spot until sunrise before making it back to camp.

There was no mention of Mikko. No explanation for why Mike or Pat didn't return for her either. She was the famous climber, and I was just a kid. Her claims cut deep. At the time, I couldn't understand how someone could rewrite reality so easily. For more than a decade, I woke up from recurring nightmares, reliving that moment, trying to make sense of it.

Her words, combined with the deaths of Alison Hargreaves, Rob Parker, Babu Chiri, and later Ang Rita, pushed me away from big public expeditions. I loved the mountains, the thrill of the climb, but not the politics, the manipulation, or the way some people were willing to step on others just to get ahead.

Another climber, Bear Grylls, spent years claiming to be the youngest Briton to summit Everest, writing books and securing a Guinness World Record he never actually held. He knew the truth, I told him myself, but that didn't matter. The story brought fame, sponsorships, and a carefully crafted public image. Meanwhile, Michael Matthews, who tragically perished on the mountain in 1999, had reached the summit at 22, still older than me. Yet, these records went unchallenged, their narratives left unchecked.

I never set out to dispute them. These were men with huge wealth, influence, and powerful connections, one chasing celebrity, the other remembered through the grief of those who loved him. The truth was irrelevant in the face of media and legacy. Over the years, plenty of younger climbers have reached the summit, making these claims obsolete. But for me, climbing was never about records. Watching the industry shift, where truth was malleable, and standing on the shoulders of pioneers became a shortcut to stardom, only deepened my disillusionment. It seemed that mountain climbing was no longer about exploring the unknown; it was about controlling the narrative.

I was very short of money so had only briefly spoken to my parents about the date and time of my arrival back into Melbourne. No one besides immediate family and a few friends had been remotely interested in my departure to Everest so I assumed it would be the same on my return. My return to Australia, however, coincided a few days before a major public holiday. With the need to fill holiday newspapers I found myself in the feature article in most national newspapers, then news items, radio and lots of public speaking. It all felt like a whirlwind, I had gone from total obscurity on a mountain to national celebrity virtually overnight. This was not the reason I climbed and my experiences were clearly a completely different world from what most people could relate to. There was one benefit though, that came via a feature article on the number one rated programme, Channel 9 News. When the attractive interviewer asked me, "So James, you have conquered the world's highest mountain, what do you plan to do next?" I replied, "Find a girlfriend." I am to this day eternally grateful to Pat for pulling up my trousers and ensuring everything remained operational.

In the years since the three of us reached the summit, awareness of mountain climbing, especially Everest, has skyrocketed. Today, it's rare to meet someone who hasn't heard of it. The commercialisation of Everest has brought both opportunities and challenges. I believe that whether people speak of Everest positively or negatively, it's always a good thing. Chomolungma, the Mother Goddess of Earth, remains a symbol of human achievement. The pollution on Everest is a reflection of what's happening in nearly every town around the world. The continued loss of life on the mountain, despite advancements like oxygen stashes and fixed lines, underscores how many nations, including my own, prioritise profit over people's safety. In time, Everest's environmental and safety improvements could set a global standard. If we can make Everest pollution-free and safe, we can do the same in the communities where we live and raise our families.

As for my friend Mike, he still cannot remember anything from the summit day through to the trip back to Base Camp. In 1996 he climbed to the summit of Mount Everest again, this time via the south side.

About the Author

James Allen grew up in a small jungle village in Nigeria, where wild landscapes and raw adventure shaped his fearless spirit. That spark led him to the highest peaks, the most unforgiving deserts, and the furthest reaches of the planet.

At 22 years old, he became the youngest Westerner to climb Everest's perilous north side, a feat that set him on a lifelong quest for discovery. He has since climbed the Seven Summits and Seven Volcanic Summits, skied to the South Pole and across Greenland, sailed vast oceans, and tackled extreme desert, Arctic, and sea kayaking expeditions. As a professional explorer, he has spent decades helping businesses, governments, and individuals push the boundaries of what's possible.

But adventure isn't just about the wild, it's about giving back.

James is the founder of "Explore by JAX", a groundbreaking platform with a mission to make adventure accessible to all, whether for a first-time hiker or a seasoned explorer. He is also a passionate advocate for environmental sustainability and social impact, believing that true exploration means protecting the planet and ensuring that everyone, homeless, orphaned, or disadvantaged, has a chance to thrive.

Above all, James is driven to inspire you, the next generation of explorers, young and old, to embrace curiosity, chase what excites you, and turn your passion into purpose.

Photo section

1 : New Zealand, 1993. Without a guidebook, Ben Palich and I (pictured) climbed tough rock and ice, often soloing avalanche slopes. We stayed unroped so if one was taken, the other could search. It saved our lives more than once.

2 : Rock climbing in Mt Arapiles, Victoria 1990.

3 : Potala Palace, Lhasa. The beauty of this place was unlike anything I had seen before. Surrounded by dirt roads, pilgrims and hundreds of bicycles (there were very few if any cars in Tibet at that time) the golden roof gleamed of resistance and hope.

4 : Driving to base camp. With only eight 4WDs in all Tibet in 1995, breakdowns were inevitable. After a few days the roads were too bad and we had to ditch the cars for a dusty, bumpy ride, sitting on our bags in the back of a military truck.

5 : Tibetan mountain boy collecting flat rock. I turned a corner and there he was, resting high up a kilometre or more above the valley floor. I liked his Chinese army hat.

6 : Tibetan girls. Two cheeky girls in a remote Tibetan village. No matter how cold or dirty they were all Tibetans were heart-warmingly friendly and excited to see people from other countries.

7 : First view of Everest. It stood like a super giant in a sea of giants. I was already struggling to breath at 5,000 metres. I remember feeling frightened but also excited. Bring it on! Rob Parker, Jeff and Mandy Dickinson helping Jeff take an old school plate photograph.

8 : Mt Everest with Himex and OTT teams from Base Camp, 5,150 metres. The North Ridge is the left skyline, West ridge right skyline. I'm hidden right hand side, back, green hat.

9 : My Base Camp home. All my clothes were borrowed or from opportunity shops. I was a mismatch of colours and sizes, Jon and Brigitte Muir's tent in the background.

10 : Yak headers helping me sew sponsorship logos onto my equipment. These guys had no shame in stealing your gear. At night, hands would appear under the fly of the tent and only disappear when you gave them a firm stab with your knife.

11 : Base camp luxury. This was a place to relax, wash and dry out gear.
I even had a pillow! It was cold though and each night the two water bottles
in my sleeping bag would freeze solid.

12 : Mt Everest from Rongbuk Monastery. The highest permanent
settlement in the world at 5,009 metres. They aerate the river to the right so
fish can survive at this height.

13 : Weighing gear for the yaks to move to Advance Base Camp.

14 : North Face, Mt Everest. We climbed the prominent ridge to the left and then under the summit. The First, Second and Third Steps can be seen silhouetted against the clouds. The plume of cloud coming off the summit is indication of high winds up high.

14 : Bob Hempstead doing rope tricks at Base Camp. Bob was the first person to do a cowboy rope trick on each of the seven summits.

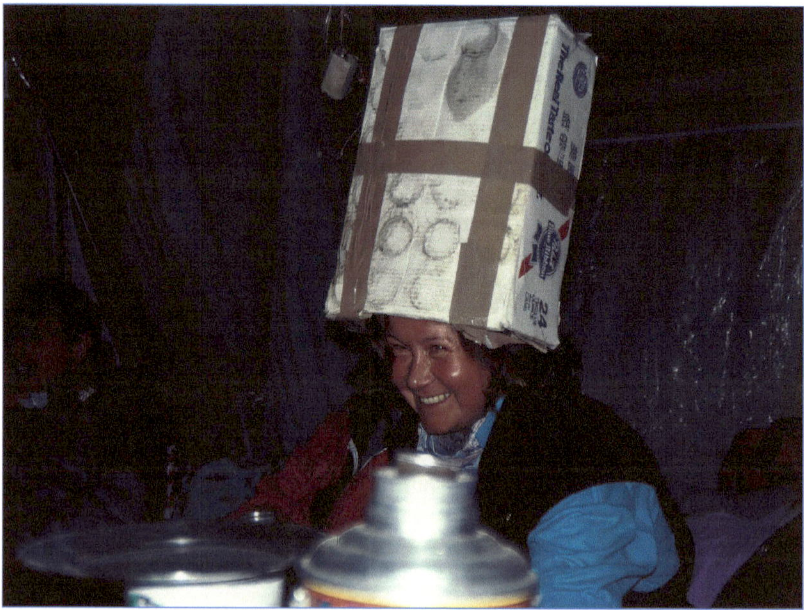

15 : Alison Hargreaves wearing her best beer hat. Dress up night at Base Camp.

16 : Base camp relaxing. Me giving a lecture on the benefits of a team calendar.

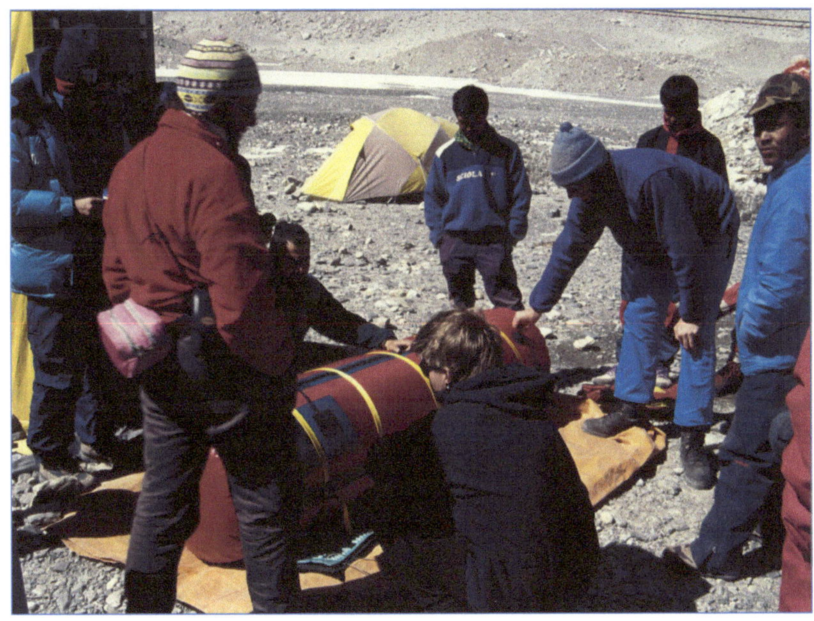

17 : The foot pump pressurized Gamo bag was the last hope for many. We used it three times on the trip and each time the climber lived. From left to right Yves (Red), Mick, Nasuh, Nima, Dorji, Graham, Babu and Jon Tinker.

18 : Advance Base Camp, 6,400 metres. Our OTT expedition to the left and Himex to the right. Kitchen tent is the large tent in the middle.

19 : Advanced Base Camp, 6,400 metres. Looking towards the North Col and ridge. Sleeping on an angle was preferable to sleeping on sharp jagged rocks.

20 : Sombrero James. It actually worked really well at keeping the strong sun off my body. This is the hat I took to the summit but then forgot to take it out of my bag for a picture.

21 : Supplying North Col. Up the fixed lines to the North Col. Avalanches regularly fell down this slope while we were there.

22 : Celebrating my 22nd birthday at North Col, 7,000 metres. Unfortunately, there wasn't enough oxygen in the air for the candle to remain alight, but I'd brought up a can of peaches … luxury.

23 : North Col tents, 7,000 metres. When we returned from the summit, a crevasse had opened up in the middle of all the tents; the left three tents were about to slide off the Col.

24 : Tent life North Col. The North Col tents were used largely as storage tents for supplies up the mountain. We slept, lived and ate on top of the ropes, tents and ice stakes.

25 : North Col looking to the North Face and North Ridge behind. From here on up we only wore down suits and you can see just how uncomfortably small this suit was on me!

26 : Snow slope to Camp 2a, 7,600 metres. This photo was taken around 7,300 metres at the end of the fixed ropes. Pat and I continued taking rope and tents higher to set up Camp 2a.

27 : Camp 2a, 7,600 metres. Looking over the tents back towards Changtse.

28 : Camp 2a, 7,600 metres. Me melting snow for a brew.

29 : Heading up towards Camp 2b looking back, 7,800 metres. Strong winds lower down.

30 : View from the tent at Camp 2b, 7,900 metres. Looking back towards the summit of Changtse before the storm.

31 : Camp 2b, 7,900 metres. I took this photo sheltering behind a rock. Moments later the tent was shredded by the approximately 200 kilometre per hour winds.

32 : Rubbish at Camp 2b, 7,900 metres. How you deal with rubbish on Everest has been a problem since the very first expeditions came to climb the mountain.

33 : Heading up the long snow slope to Camp 3. Pat is in the foreground, Changste behind him and on the horizon Base Camp way down the valley (top right of centre).

34 : Climbing up the rock and ice gullies towards Camp 3. Cloud plumes can be seen coming off the summit behind.

35 : Camp 3, approx. 8,200 metres. Looking up towards Russell's tent with my tent on the right. The First Step, Second Step, Third Step and Summit are all visible from this position.

36 : First Step, approx. 8,500 metres. Looking back uphill towards the First Step with Niama and Mike in foreground (taken on the way down).

37 : Ridge between First Step and Second Step, approx. 8,550 metres. For some reason I cut left over the ledge and along rather than remaining high. Pat centre to left of the snow.

38 : Second Step, approx. 8,600 metres. Mike resting at the top of the first rock shelf (centre) after falling down the face (taken on the way down).

39 : The final snow pyramid, 8,600 metres. The summit seems so close yet it's a long slow slog up the hard snow. We traversed right below the top onto the North Face rock face.

40 : The summit rises on the final ridge to the summit. Mike up ahead.

41 : Me on the summit of Mt Everest, 8,848.13 metres. Halfway there.

42 : Summit prayer flags. Mike on left and Pat behind. The Taiwanese team had left the metal poles you see. Apparently, they were used to accurately measure the height with lasers.

43 : Mike making the summit radio call. He collapsed moments later. You can just make out his solar panel.

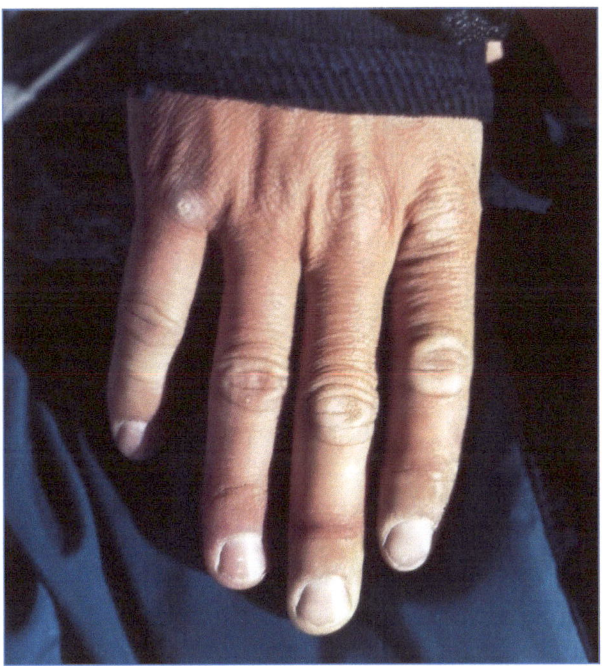

44 : "Allen rings"—the first photo of my frostbite. I took this at the base of the Second Step. You can see the yellow rings at the top of the third joint on my index and middle finger. By the time I made it to base camp a day and a half later, they'd turned black.

45 : Pat and me back at Advanced Base Camp. I lost more than 35 kilograms over the course of the trip.

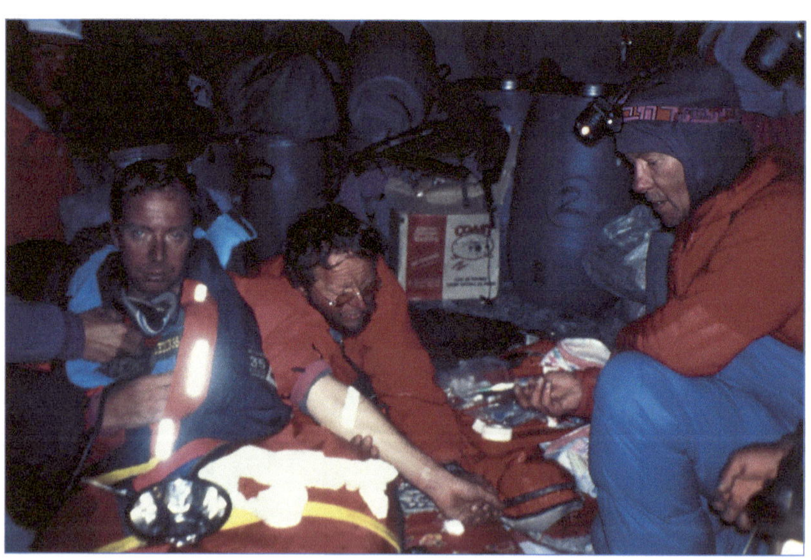

46 : Mike at Advanced Base Camp. Doctors around Mike, Kelly to the left (out of shot), Yves and Dick Price.

47 : Russell helping clean and slowly warm my frostbitten fingers.
I kept my hand in this bucket for a while before I got bored and went off to
see Mike.

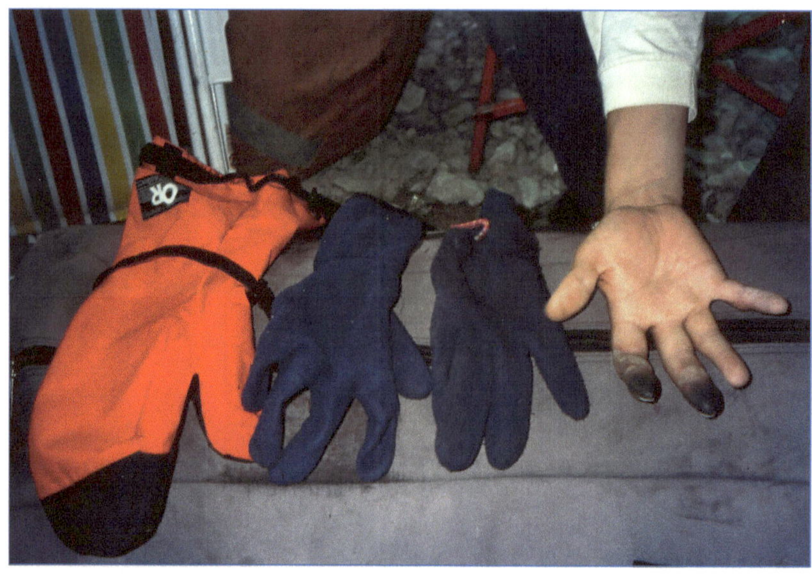

48 : The two layers of gloves (right) that I had on over my fingers when I got frostbite and the windshell I removed (left). The two frostbitten fingers touched metal for a minute before getting frozen.

49 : The Base Camp afterparty. Darts, drinks and over $US1,000 of fireworks fired horizontally. What a day and night to remember that was!